HOW TO READ LITERATURE LIKE A PROFESSOR

Thomas C. Foster

AUTHORED by Sheza Alqera Atiq
UPDATED AND REVISED by Aaron Suduiko

COVER DESIGN by Table XI Partners LLC
COVER PHOTO by Olivia Verma and © 2005 GradeSaver, LLC

BOOK DESIGN by Table XI Partners LLC

Published by GradeSaver LLC, www.gradesaver.com

First published in the United States of America by GradeSaver LLC. 2015

GRADESAVER, the GradeSaver logo and the phrase "Getting you the grade since 1999" are registered trademarks of GradeSaver, LLC

ISBN 978-1-60259-570-5

Printed in the United States of America

For other products and additional information please visit http://www.gradesaver.com

Table of Contents

Biography of Thomas C. Foster (circa 1952–)

Thomas C. Foster has served as at the University of Michigan, Flint for 28 years, teaching courses on literature and writing as Professor of English. Foster is also Director of the Master of English Language and Literature program at the University.

Having grown up in West Cornfield, Michigan, Foster found his closest companions were books rather than classmates, sparking a love for literature that has lasted to this day. His earliest interests included works by Robert Louis Stevenson and Mark Twain, and his present academic writing concentrates on twentieth-century British, American and Irish figures and movements. Foster attended Dartmouth College where he concentrated on English, graduating with High Distinction in the major in 1974. He pursued English further in Michigan State University, progressing from eighteenth and nineteenth century literary works to twentieth century writing. He obtained his masters and doctorate in the subject in 1977 and 1981 respectively.

Although Foster's current research focuses on figures such as James Joyce, William Faulkner, Seamus Heaney, John Fowles, Derek Mahon, Eavan Boland, and the modernist and postmodernist movements, he reads and teaches on several other literary branches. These include writers such as Shakespeare, Dickens, Hardy, Twain, Homer, Poe, Ibsen, and Sophocles.

In addition to *How to Read Novels Like a Professor* (Summer 2008) and *How to Read Literature Like a Professor* (2003), published through HarperCollins, Foster is the author of *Form and Society in Modern Literature* (Northern Illinois University Press, 1988), *Seamus Heaney* (Twayne, 1989), and *Understanding John Fowles* (University of South Carolina Press, 1994). His novel, *The Professor's Daughter*, is in progress.

Foster has noted that he has learned more about literature through his students than through all the classes he has taken on the subject during his educational career.

How to Read Literature Like a Professor Study Guide

How To Read English Like a Professor: A Lively and Entertaining Guide to Reading Between the Lines, published by HarperCollins in 2003, was well-received by audiences, and continues to enjoy a place on the New York Times bestseller list for Education. In light of the work's popularity, the author, Thomas C. Foster, followed his book with the sequels, *How to Read Novels Like a Professor* in 2008 and *How To Read English Like A Professor for Kids* in 2013.

How To Read draws heavily on the author's experience as a professor of English - indeed, the book is geared towards students of literature that hope to better understand the analytical process that often takes place in the classrooms and by the teachers. The work is constructed on the age-old idea that books and writing are seldom original - and that, in fact, to get the most out of one's reading experience one has to train oneself to detect patterns, symbolism and historical links all of which are contained in a literary work. Foster illustrates this concept by setting forth key themes and indicators which he finds to be most fundamental to literary reading and analysis, through an approach that is less scholarly and more personal. This instruction manual for students of literature frequently cites works of great fiction and classics so as to provide references for the author's arguments, even concluding with an analysis of a particular twentieth century short story.

The books has been well received by reviewers, lauded particularly by educationalists who have found Foster's work helpful for suggesting novel approaches to reading and making accessible the process of engagement with literature. Many have expressed appreciation of the "Lively and Entertaining" voice of the work, finding that the title lives up to its promise of delivering an engaging read. The work has not, however, been without its criticism. For example, Alan Jacobs, author and Professor, has criticized *How to Read* by challenging the premise that reading is best done with a highly trained or professional eye, and emphasizes instead the value of reading for pleasure. With a field as complex and vast as literary theory and analysis, judgments on the more elemental characteristics of fictive writing are far from conclusive. Foster himself has admitted to receiving criticism and competing interpretations from his readers, and acknowledges that the ideas presented in his work are subjective and not necessarily comprehensive of literary tools and features.

How to Read Literature Like a Professor Summary

How to Read English Like a Professor: A Lively and Entertaining Guide to Reading Between the Lines is a nonfiction literary guide that aims to assist readers and students in their engagement with literature. The book identifies certain literary conventions that guide literature; knowledge of and familiarity with these conventions would enable a beginner reader to become a professional one, and read literature as professors do. A basic premise of the book is that there are different reading levels that range from basic response level to more in depth analysis. Becoming a professional reader entails learning how to read analytically, and the author Thomas C. Foster sets out key characteristics of literature that can aid in developing these analytical skills.

These characteristics - or literary elements - are numerous and while Foster doesn't purport to present all in his guide, he highlights ones that are believed to be most essential. Thus, the book identifies traditions and older texts that literature borrows heavily from and contains allusions to such as Shakespeare, the Bible, Greek mythology, and Fairytales. In addition to considering external influences, *How to Read* also focuses on elements within the text such as setting, weather, organizational structure (Sonnet), as well as particular themes including blindness, food, supernatural creatures, flight and irony. Thus the conventions considered by the book range from external historic texts, to thematic concerns and finally to text specific features.

Along the way the author also considers broader questions of what literature is, how and why we react to it, the creative process, and the purpose of reading itself. He concludes by an analysis of Katherine Mansfield's short story, "The Garden Party," to provide, by way of example, professorial reading and analysis - a practical application of the points set forth in the book.

How to Read Literature Like a Professor Characters

Thomas C. Foster

Narrator and Author of the *How to Read English Like A Professor* guide.

How to Read Literature Like a Professor Glossary

Veritable

True or Real. Being in fact the thing named and not false, unreal, or imaginary —often used to stress the aptness of a metaphor. <a *veritable* mountain of references>

"Veritable." *Merriam-Webster.com*. Merriam-Webster, n.d. Web. 22 July 2015. <http://www.merriam-webster.com/dictionary/veritable>.

Liturgical

Of or relating to liturgy; a fixed set of ceremonies, words, etc., that are used during public worship in a religion.

"Liturgy." *Merriam-Webster.com*. Merriam-Webster, n.d. Web. 22 July 2015. <http://www.merriam-webster.com/dictionary/liturgy>.

Apocryphal

Well-known but probably not true. Of doubtful authenticity.

"Apocryphal." *Merriam-Webster.com*. Merriam-Webster, n.d. Web. 22 July 2015. <http://www.merriam-webster.com/dictionary/apocryphal>

Dictum

A statement or well-known remark that expresses an important idea or rule. A formal pronouncement of a principle, proposition, or opinion or an observation intended or regarded as authoritative.

"Dictum." *Merriam-Webster.com*. Merriam-Webster, n.d. Web. 22 July 2015. <http://www.merriam-webster.com/dictionary/dictum>.

Villanelle

A chiefly French verse form running on two rhymes and consisting typically of five tercets (i.e., a unit or group of 3-line verse) and a quatrain in which the first and third lines of the opening tercet recur alternately at the end of the other tercets and together as the last two lines of the quatrain.

"Villanelle." *Merriam-Webster.com*. Merriam-Webster, n.d. Web. 22 July 2015. <http://www.merriam-webster.com/dictionary/villanelle>.

Allegory

A literary feature that seeks to convey a particular meaning or message. Symbols of ideas of human experience or political/historical situation.

Fecundity

- Fruitful/productive in offspring or vegetation

- Intellectually productive or inventive to a marked degree

"Fecund." *Merriam-Webster.com*. Merriam-Webster, n.d. Web. 22 July 2015. <http://www.merriam-webster.com/dictionary/fecund>.

Titular

Having an important or impressive title but not having the power or duties that usually go with it. Existing in title only.

"Titular." *Merriam-Webster.com*. Merriam-Webster, n.d. Web. 22 July 2015. <http://www.merriam-webster.com/dictionary/titular>.

Malefactor

Someone who is guilty of a crime or offense : a person whose behavior is wrong or evil.

"Malefactor." *Merriam-Webster.com*. Merriam-Webster, n.d. Web. 22 July 2015. <http://www.merriam-webster.com/dictionary/malefactor>

Narrative Misdirection

A situation when the author leads the reader to emotionally identify with a character causing him/her to see things only or largely through that characters' perspective - at times at the risk of ignoring/misunderstanding reality.

Example: strong affinity for the character of Harry in Harry Potter.

Habitué

A person who is often at a specified place.

"Habitué." *Merriam-Webster.com.* Merriam-Webster, n.d. Web. 22 July 2015. <http://www.merriam-webster.com/dictionary/habitué>.

Gnomon

An object that by the position or length of its shadow serves as an indicator especially of the hour of the day. Example, a pin of a sundial or column erected perpendicular to horizon.

"Gnomon." *Merriam-Webster.com.* Merriam-Webster, n.d. Web. 22 July 2015. <http://www.merriam-webster.com/dictionary/gnomon>.

Verisimilitude

The quality of seeming real.

"Verisimilitude." *Merriam-Webster.com.* Merriam-Webster, n.d. Web. 22 July 2015. <http://www.merriam-webster.com/dictionary/verisimilitude>.

Machismo

An attitude, quality, or way of behaving that agrees with traditional ideas about men being very strong and aggressive.

"Machismo." *Merriam-Webster.com.* Merriam-Webster, n.d. Web. 22 July 2015. <http://www.merriam-webster.com/dictionary/machismo>

Repartee

a: a quick and witty reply.

b : a succession or interchange of clever retorts : amusing and usually light sparring with words.

"Repartee." *Merriam-Webster.com*. Merriam-Webster, n.d. Web. 22 July 2015. <http://www.merriam-webster.com/dictionary/repartee>.

Irony

In literary contexts: a deflection from expectation.

When the audience understands something that eludes one or more of the characters.

Sordid

Characterized by baseness. Filthy, in the metaphoric or literal sense

Antecedent

In literary context:

a) A preceding event, condition, or cause

b) The significant events, conditions, and traits of one's earlier life

c) The people in a family who lived in past times

"Antecedent." *Merriam-Webster.com*. Merriam-Webster, n.d. Web. 22 July 2015. <http://www.merriam-webster.com/dictionary/antecedent>.

Ionian/Aegean

Ionian: a member of any of the Greek peoples who settled on the islands of the Aegean Sea and the western shore of Asia Minor toward the end of the second millennium b.c.

Aegean: of or relating to the arm of the Mediterranean Sea east of Greece. Of or relating to the chiefly Bronze Age civilization of the islands of the Aegean Sea and the countries adjacent to it.

"Ionian." *Merriam-Webster.com*. Merriam-Webster, n.d. Web. 22 July 2015.
<http://www.merriam-webster.com/dictionary/Ionian>

"Aegean." *Merriam-Webster.com*. Merriam-Webster, n.d. Web. 22 July 2015.
<http://www.merriam-webster.com/dictionary/Aegean>.

Modernism

A style of art, architecture, literature, etc., that uses ideas and methods which are very different from those used in the past. A self-conscious break from the past.

"Modernism." *Merriam-Webster.com*. Merriam-Webster, n.d. Web. 22 July 2015.
<http://www.merriam-webster.com/dictionary/modernism>.

Postmodernism

Of, relating to, or being any of various movements in reaction to modernism that are typically characterized by ironic self-reference and absurdity (as in literature).

"Postmodern." *Merriam-Webster.com*. Merriam-Webster, n.d. Web. 22 July 2015.
<http://www.merriam-webster.com/dictionary/postmodern>.

How to Read Literature Like a Professor Themes

Creative Imagination

Foster describes the process of reading as the engagement of one creative imagination with another. The terms "creative imagination" appear to suggest a freethinking approach that knows no boundaries - the reality, as the author argues, is in fact quite different. In employing our creative imaginations we work within the parameters set out in the text, to freely inquire about the possible meanings and associations related to the images, characters, and events. Our affective response to a writing synthesizes this process - we respond or relate to certain aspects of the writing and it is in trying to understand the meaning that such features hold for us, whilst also attempting to discover the possible meanings the writer had in mind whilst writing the piece, that we allow literature to harness our capacity for creative imagination.

Memory, symbolism and pattern are features of literary analysis that can help maximize this potential.. Foster is keen to point out the interconnectedness of all literary works (see intertextuality below) a characteristic that the reader can quickly use to his/her advantage as he/she peruses a range of texts. *Symbolism* is also inherent to literature - the key notion that the language and writing contained in the work actually stands in for something else. These can take several shapes and forms - metaphor, analogy, signified/signifier - but they all ultimately allude to the fact that more often than not in literature there is more than what meets the eye. Foster describes awareness of literary symbolism as "a predisposition to seeing things as existing in themselves while simultaneously also representing something else." Understanding *patterns* that run through literary works helps tie all these characteristics together, and prepares the reader to be much more conscious of what he/she is reading. In discerning patterns we understand the elements that characterize a certain storyline, character or events, paving the way for a far more engaged imagination.

Foster puts this succinctly when he states, "Much of what we think about literature, we feel first. Having instincts, though, doesn't automatically mean they work at their highest level...The more you exercise the symbolic imagination, the better and quicker it works" (P 106-107 Chapter 12, Is That A Symbol?).

Intertextuality

Intertextuality refers to connections that often lie between works of literature. An intertextual literary analysis focuses on the complex interrelationship between a text and other texts as central to the interpretation and understanding of the work in question. A basic premise of literature is that each literary work builds upon another - a fact aptly voiced by T.S Eliot, whom the author quotes as describing new works of literature as adding to and altering an order of monuments which already stand.

Intertextuality is believed to enrich the reading experience, bringing in multiple layers of meaning which the reader may not have been conscious of. Dialogue between different texts allow the reader to make comparisons and draw parallels which shifts the focus above and beyond what is overtly presented in a particular literary piece.

Parody

The use of parody typically presents a character or thing (or place) in a humorous light. The mode in which parody is employed can take on varying forms - the effect can range from amusing to ridiculous. Parody is also used to refer to cases where the writing is a (deliberately) poor or feeble imitation of someone or something. Often however, parody means to provide entertainment or amusement for the reader through mimicry.

Foster describes how parody can be used when a literary work contains references to another (the intertextual dialogue). Foster cites John Fowles as an example - the author in parodies the writing of his predecessor, Henry James and the Victorian novel tradition in his work, "The French Lieutenant's Woman." Foster also explains Salman Rushdie's novel, "The Satanic Verses" in terms of parody describing how, "When Salman Rushdie wrote The Satanic Verses (1988), he caused his characters to parody (in order to show their wickedness, among other things) certain events and persons from the Koran and the life of the Prophet" (p 52-53). See 'Interlude' and Chapter 7, '...Or the Bible.'

Form and Structural Analysis

Foster devotes an entire chapter to Sonnet (Chapter 4, If It's Square, It's a Sonnet) to illustrate the significance of form to a literary work, particularly poetry. He points out that scholars and critics often study form because it is so deliberate - the crafting of a poem under a certain rhyme scheme or structure is careful work, and is usually carried out for certain desired effect. The physicality of the literary piece, then, comes to have as much significance as the text and content itself.

A sonnet is a poem of fourteen lines written in iambic pentameter using a number of rhyme schemes. Typically this scheme tends to be around 10 syllables per line. A student of literature is often encouraged to look at the parts where the line or syllable breaks of or transitions to another - how this affects the sentence, and what it might mean for the author to choose to place a certain word or imagery in a certain place.

Closely associated with sonnet is iambic pentameter - a line of verse with five metrical feet, each consisting of one short (or unstressed) syllable followed by one long (or stressed) syllable.

The example provided by Foster is Christina Rossetti's "An Echo From Willow Wood" and in analyzing the poem he explains how the rhyme scheme "reinforces the basic concept...The beauty of this poem, lies, in part, in the tension between the small package and the large emotional and narrative scene it contains...The vessel, the sonnet form, actually becomes part of the meaning of the poem" (p 27).

Scriptural and Biblical Interpretation

Many works of literature - from premodern to Victorian to postmodernist texts - draw on Biblical or scriptural imagery. Foster describes the prevalence of Christian imagery and direct or indirect biblical quotations in poetry, novels and short stories to emphasize the importance of reading literature through such lens. Of course the inclusion of such imagery and reference is independent of the religiosity of the author in question - as Foster points out, "since the preponderance of cultural influences has come down to us from European early settlers, and since these settlers inflicted their values on the "benighted" cultures they encountered...those inflicted values have gained ascendancy" (p 117).

Biblical or Christian imagery in a work of literature inevitably alludes to certain values but the values do not have to be inherently religious. They are often more pertinent in revealing some aspect of the society presented in the literature, and achieves this in various ways whether by commenting on gender roles, the individual's role in society, or humankind's relation to nature. Biblical references thus might suggest continuation of the tradition (or aspects of the tradition)

Reader-Response Literary Theory

In literary theory, the reader-response analysis focuses on the reader's interaction with the text in question. Such an approach pays attention to the reader's experience of the literary work, and believes that it is the reader that 'completes' a meaning of the text through his/her own interpretation. The reading process is thus considered as significant in shedding light on the meaning of the work as the writing itself.

Although not explicitly acknowledging this particular approach in literary analysis, Foster implicitly stresses its importance in his work. The author says, for instance, "We tend to give writers all the credit, but reading is also an event of the imagination; our creativity, our inventiveness, encounters that of the writer and in that meeting we puzzle out what she means, what we understand her to mean, what uses we can put her writing to." (p 107, Chapter 12: Is That A Symbol? Also see 'Creative Imagination' above.)

Irony

The use of irony in literature is defined as,

"a technique of indicating, as through character or plot development, an intention or attitude opposite to that which is actually or ostensibly stated."

and in contemporary writing as,

" a manner of organizing a workso as to give full expression to contradictory or complementary impulses, attitudes, etc., especially as a means of indicating detachment from a subject, theme, or emotion" (Dictionary.com).

If an author is writing in the ironic mode, the reader should take care to understand that another, possibly alternative meaning, underlies the writing or description. For Foster, irony involves "a deflection from expectation," and also says, "...irony works because the audience understands something that eludes one or more of the characters." (Chapter 26, Is He Serious? And Other Ironies). Thus it is all the more significant for the reader to be cautious in his/her interpretation of the literary work. Irony as a literary tool is especially prevalent in modernist and postmodern literature.

How to Read Literature Like a Professor Quotes and Analysis

"In literature there is no better, no more lyrical, no more perfectly metaphorical illness than heart disease."

Foster (p 208, Chapter 23)

Here the author describes how heart disease is a favorite trope employed by writers because of its rather straightforward nature, as well as the implications inherent in the act. As the seat of emotion, and even character, the heart becomes symbolic of several themes of significance to personality and life. A heart disease is not only a quick and easy way to dispose off characters writers want killed, but it is also a meaningful one.

"...as soon as we notice blindness and sight as thematic components of a work, more and more related images and phrases emerge in the text."

Foster (p 203, Chapter 22)

Foster stresses the symbolism and meaning attached to a blind character in a work of literature. Writers choose to blind characters for more than the simple reason of highlighting the phenomenon of blindness - considerable complexity is attached with this condition which requires a shift in perspective not only of the blind figure in question, but all those around him who have to change or act in ways that consider this characteristic.

Blindness is heavily metaphorical and for this reason is often associated with issues of truth, light, understanding and so forth. Related imagery can include shadows, darkness, obscurity, words/writing, hearing, etc.

"...irony works because the audience understands something that eludes one or more of the characters".

Foster (p 240, Chapter 26)

If a work makes use of irony, then the reader should be careful not to take things at face value. Indeed, as the quote suggests, irony often involves a realization or message that is distinct from what is traditionally thought or expected.

When a work is written in an ironic mode then often characters in the story are unable to realize reality for what it is or understand consequences of their actions/behavior/comprehension. In this case they have less independence or free will than might otherwise exist in a work that is not ironical and where the audience is more or less on the same page as the character.

"Never feel dumb. Not knowing who or what is ignorance, which is no sin; ignorance is simply the measure of what you haven't got to yet."

Foster (p 283, Appendix Reading List)

In his concluding statements Foster points out how engagement with literature and our position as professional readers is an ongoing process. We will never be able to exhaust the literary conventions that exist nor perhaps know all cases of symbolism yet that ignorance should never deter us from studying more literature, or reading more books. There is something to be gained from each reading, and even the most professional of literary scholars stand to learn something new each time they interact with a text or author.

"Instead try to find a reading perspective that allows for sympathy with the historical moment of the story, that understands the text as having been written against its own social, historical, cultural, and personal background."

Foster (p 228, Chapter 25)

Foster explains the importance of contextualizing a work of literature when attempting to understand its possible layers of meaning or analyzing it. It is important, in other words, for readers not to be blinded by their present contexts and worldview - for the conditions in which the author of the work penned the story was likely quite distinct from the ones we currently experience. Doing so would lead to greater insights into the text, and allow for a richer interaction.

Foster also cautions against adopting a completely impartial perspective - he stresses that instinctive responses during initial readings are just as, if not the most, important in leading to subsequent analysis and deeper engagement. One has to learn, however, to maintain a balance between recognizing one's personal responses and considering the period and environment in which the work was compiled.

"That one story that has been going on forever is all around us. We - as readers or writers, tellers or listeners - understand each other, we share knowledge of the structures of our myths, we comprehend the logic of symbols, largely because we have access to the same swirl of story"

Foster (p 192, Interlude)

Much of Foster's book is based on the premise that ultimately, there is only one story about the experience of being human. Literature, in other words, is an attempt to present, capture, and narrate the experience of living in this world, how we behave, what meaning we give to the elements around us, how we are influenced in turn by the world we are residing in, and so on. Because we have among us different tribes, people, communities rather than a single nation or race, this experience of being human is multifaceted and complex. As a result different variations of this single story inevitably exist.

These variations that can be contained in storytelling or myth, have transcended boundaries since the beginning of time and the more enduring or popular ones have becomes ingrained in our collective consciousness. As a result while we might encounter different texts or stories, because of our shared experience as humans as well as this collective consciousness, we can relate and make sense of the narrations we come across. Part of learning to become a professional reader, for Foster, is simply learning to be more attuned and conscious of these large traditions of which we are a part.

> *"What we mean in speaking of "myth" in general is story, the ability of story to explain ourselves to ourselves in ways that physics, philosophy, mathematics, chemistry - all very highly useful and informative in their own right - can't. That explanation takes the shape of stories that are deeply ingrained in our group memory, that shape our culture and are in turn shaped by it, that constitute a way of seeing by which we read the world, and, ultimately, ourselves."*

> *Foster (p 65, Chapter 9)*

"Myth" as used by Foster does not refer to a belief or story that is untrue. Rather, it is used in the book to identify an established tradition of narrations (oral or written) that comment upon human experiences and lives. Through tales, myths can help us see and understand our lives in ways that traditional sciences may not allow.

Foster is specifically referring to a kind of myth that has endured over the centuries. Because of its popularity, or other historic factors, this myth has become so closely tied to our social fabric that we grow up with them often without realizing that we do. Examples of such enduring traditions or body of stories include Biblical mythology, Greco-Roman traditions, Shakespearean stories and so forth. A student of literature would benefit from a familiarity and recognition of such myths because of how heavily literature - at least Western and European literature - is indebted to it.

> *"That world contains many things, and on the level of society, part of what it contains is the political reality of the time - power structures, relations among classes, issues of justice and rights, interactions between the sexes and among various racial and ethnic constituencies."*

> *Foster (p 115, Chapter 13)*

Foster encourages readers to consider literature as a political work. He defends this position by pointing out how literature is inevitably a commentary on the world we live, and since our societies, lives, and environments are strongly affected by politics, so too is literature. Politics here doesn't have to refer to the ruling political party or the state of the assembly/congress; politics makes its way in institutions such as the judiciary, law, even in relationships between sex, races, and classes. Thus, a story that focuses on the differences between the upper and lower classes of a society also tell us, if implicitly, the type of political ideology and interests that are upheld in the country/region.

How to Read Literature Like a Professor Quotes and Analysis

"In a sense, every story or poem is a vacation, and every writer has to ask, every time, Where is this one taking place?"

Foster (p 163-164, Chapter 19)

Geography matters in literature because setting is one of the most important decisions that a writer takes when compiling his story. This conscious selection of place means that the setting in question has some significance whether historic, geographical, social, or other. Whether a narrative is set in a war-down city or in a prairie invariably affects the story that emerges. Each location has its own implications - the South with its tropical climates might suggest laid-back, undeveloped, poor whilst mountains might suggest exclusivity, isolation, coldness, inspiring and so forth. Setting or geography then makes a story as much as its characters or narration do, and it is worth considering possible significance of the place where this story is taking place.

"We have to bring our imaginations to bear on a story if we are to see all its possibilities; otherwise it's just about somebody who did something."

Foster (p 123, Chapter 14)

Here Foster points out how literary elements often don't fall into neat categories — different writers, for instance, can manipulate symbols and archetypes in different ways. If a text contains allusions to a Christ figure then one should not expect the corresponding character in the text to embody all, or even most of the qualities traditionally associated with this archetype. A writer may simply choose to focus on highlighting the character's sense of benevolence, or sacrifice, when drawing parallels between the two figures rather than in making the character embody all saintly qualities. This then is what the author describes as "seeing" all possibilities inherent in a literary work, and being open minded enough if we come across a striking image or characteristic so as to create room for both the writer's, as well as our own, creative imaginations.

How to Read Literature Like a Professor Introduction Summary and Analysis

Summary:

In his introduction, Thomas Foster sets out for the reader reasons why the book was written, and why it might prove to be helpful to the reader of literature. *How To Read Literature Like an English Professor* is an instructional guide that hopes to enrich the reading experience by pointing out cues that make a work of literature what it is. The introduction is thus an overall summary of these cues, as well as an account of the techniques of interpretation and analysis employed by Professors and professional students of literature.

Foster opens the chapter by recalling a classroom experience where the students couldn't understand why and how he had reached a certain conclusion about a character in Lorraine Hansberry's *A Raisin in the Sun* (1959). Foster's primary intent in referencing this text and its characters Mr. Lindner and Walter Lee Young is to show how many layers of meaning are often embedded in a text. Although *A Raisin in the Sun* is set in 20th century Chicago, the characters and plot of this modernist American play contain traces of a German legend that dates back to the 15th century (if not older). Such a connection is not apparent to Foster's students, however, which is why they are surprised when their Professor draws parallels to the Faust legend and bargains with the devil. Yet Foster argues that his theory is not unfounded, and in explaining the connections, demonstrates the complexity contained in a single literary work.

In light of such complexity literary analysis requires a certain amount of effort and training that is not immediately at hand to the beginner reader or student of literature. Foster explains this by arguing that a literary work has its own set of grammar or rules, much the same way that language itself has. The experienced reader or Professor has, over time, and through extensive reading, learnt to identify the codes and conventions and patterns that make up these rules. The way to learn to identify these cues is simply to practice - reading more and more works and becoming aware of the underlying principles that guide works of literature.

Foster distinguishes between the beginner reader and the experienced one by comparing their reading experience - the former reacts to the book or text on an affective level, also called the response level, where the reader reacts emotionally or instinctively to events, characters and development. The experienced reader on the other hand, in addition to experiencing the affective response to a work, also remains cognizant of other elements at play, asking questions such as "Where did that effect come from? Whom does this character resemble? Where have I seen this situation before?" (p xv, Introduction).

According to Foster command over three key features of literary works is what distinguishes the professional from the novice: memory, symbol and pattern. Memory involves recollection of previous works studies or read that might spur the reader to make connections between works, symbolism is a mantra that prevents the reader from taking things merely on face value, whilst identification of patterns within a work enable the reader to distance him/herself from the text even as they engage with it, to take a broader and clearer perspective of things.

In addition to these techniques, Foster explains his intention to further elucidate features of writing that would help the reader understand a text in a much deeper sense than he/she might otherwise have without prior knowledge of how literature works.

Analysis:

Foster's guide works on the premise that literature, like sciences or social sciences, requires a certain set of skills and 'training' in order to be best appreciated. While this impression is perhaps unsurprising from an academic point of view, *How To Read*, as the title suggests, is directed towards readers of literary works in general. It is not wholly clear who Foster's readers are - whether he intends the work to be used primarily by students across fields or anyone interested in picking up a book. This distinction is important, for it has implications on how one should regard literature, its role and purpose, or at least how the author regard the field.

The idea that one should "learn" how to read literature is not without its critics - Alan Jacobs, scholar of literature and literary critic has challenged the view that one has to develop a professionally trained eye in order to attain richer levels of reading experience. Author of *The Pleasures of Reading in An Age of Distraction*, Jacobs emphasizes the value of reading for one's own sake and pleasure - and seems to privilege the "affective" or "response level" of reading that Foster encourages readers to move beyond. The debate is complex, and not easily resolved, but it is significant for the reader of *How To Read* to understand the perspective and judgments that its author carries regarding the discipline of literature.

The opening of Foster's introduction - with a recollection of a classroom experience with students - is characteristic of the style the author has adopted throughout the work. The personal and directly engaging tone is undoubtedly deliberate, intending to fulfill the promise that the title carries of being a "lively and entertaining guide." Indeed reviewers and teachers have often focused on this quality of the writing in their praise for Foster's work - the jocular and informal style makes the text more accessible for the young student or reader.

Yet the informality or liveliness of the narrative voice cannot be said to apply to the work in its entirety - during analyses and explications of literary works and techniques Foster often presents arguments in a more formal manner, frequently employing literary jargon. How accessible the book truly is for its reader is thus largely contingent on the reader's own comfort in interacting with the text.

Foster's elucidation of the three key techniques that are important for meaningful literary analysis (memory, symbol, pattern) draws heavily on the theme of intertextuality. Intertextuality is used to refer to ways in which a text gains meaning by referencing or evoking other texts, what Foster calls "a dialogue" between works of literature. Often intertextual features work as subthemes or double narratives in a work. Knowingly or unwittingly writing is closely interconnected, and because of this network of literary production tools such as memory, symbolism and pattern can be applied to considerable effect. If one actively learns to keep in mind the texts read before and draw parallels whenever encountering a new work in addition to analyzing the material contained in the work itself, then it is possible to better understand what the text stands for and hone one's analytical skills.

How to Read Literature Like a Professor Chapters 1 - 3 Summary and Analysis

Summary:

Foster chooses to discuss the quest motif first, indicating that this feature is often one of the more fundamental conventions of literature. The significance of the quest can perhaps be gauged by the fact that it is associated with any trip or journey described in a text or undertaken by a character. Foster defends this position first by laying out in broad terms the stages that make up a quest, and then describing how any significant trip written about is simply a modification or form of these basic stages. Foster explains what a quest consists of first by drawing on traditional, medieval terminology and then in more general terms.

Typical perceptions of a quest involve a knight, a dangerous path, a Holy Grail, a dragon, an evil knight, and a princess. After setting out these characters Foster proceeds to analyze the features that make up a quest in more structural terms - the quest then consists of a quester, a place to go, a stated reason to go to that place, challenges and obstacles en route, and the real reason to go there. Foster points out that the real reason for a quest never involves the explicitly stated reason presented in text, rather, the real reason is always related to self-knowledge and the process of discovery.

To illustrate how the quest can take on many shapes and forms, Foster analyzes the storyline of *Crying of Lot 49*, a twentieth-century novel by Thomas Pynchon. *Crying of Lot 49* certainly doesn't fit into traditional images of the quest motif - instead of a knight, the protagonist is a young married woman, her trip takes place in modern California and her challenges or dragons include amongst other things, a mentally unstable therapist and a possible postal conspiracy. Despite such differences, Foster argues that the book is essentially a quest novel whereby the protagonist's stated goal for travel fades away and concludes with a profound shift in perception and understanding of the self. One of the most telling features of the story, according to Foster, is the character's name, Oedipa, which goes back to the tragic figure of Oedipus the King (ca. 425 B.C) whose true failure was that he didn't know himself.

Foster concludes the chapter by acknowledging that in some cases a trip can simply be a trip, that is, it doesn't have to have any deeper meaning such as that associated with a quest, but it is valuable for the reader to be alert when encountering a journey of any kind.

The second chapter discusses the literary significance of meals. More specifically, the act of eating together can be read as an act of communion. Foster is quick to point out, however, that 'communion' may not necessarily involve the traditional, Christian acts we associate with the term, but can be interpreted in literature in a variety of ways. The crucial thing to remember about communions is that it is meant to be an act of sharing and peace or goodwill. A personal act such as breaking bread that is shared with others necessarily implies a certain intimacy, friendship, connection. Foster also states that the act of describing a meal scene is a challenging task for the writer - and if it is included in a literary work then there have to be significant reasons for it.

To describe how varied literary interpretations of communion can be, Foster draws on the meal scenes presented in Henry Fielding's *Tom Jones* (1749) and Raymond Carver's *Cathedral* (1981). The first includes a dine-in at an inn where Tom and Mrs. Walters devour their meal unabashedly. Although the setting and thematic positioning of the meal doesn't appear to be significant or indicative of traditional notions of communion, it nonetheless involves a shared experience of desire. In the movie version the decadent scene is actually a stand-in for a sexual experience between the two characters. In Cathedral, on the other hand, where a blind man is invited for dinner, the meal becomes an opportunity for the protagonist to overcome his biases against certain people and identify, through eating together, the qualities that reveal the humanity of his comrade and the similarities in their experience of life.

Foster also considers situations where a meal takes an unpleasant turn, or doesn't happen at all. Such cases are just as significant for they indicate clearly to the reader a certain wrong or injustice that is being orchestrated through the violation of the principle of respecting the ones with whom you break bread. Foster references Anne Tyler's *Dinner at the Homesick Restaurant* (1982) and James Joyce's "The Dead" (1914) to illustrate how even tense or late dinner parties can still be symbolic of communion, and how, in each cases, the characters are brought together, in a literal and metaphoric sense, around the dinner table.

In chapter three Foster discusses the literary significance of the use of fantastic or supernatural figures such as vampires and ghosts. According to Foster, such figures in literary texts are rarely only used to give readers a scare. Instead, they are often also symbolic of darker principles such as exploitation, selfishness, domination and so forth. Foster draws upon the classic example of *Dracula* (1897) to demonstrate how the Vampire's attack on young women is closely related to themes of seduction, unwholesome lust, and danger not to mention other evils. Figures such as Dracula or ghosts then are foreboding markers that indicate to the reader how amiss state of affairs are, on a human character as well as social level. Such darkly fantastic creatures are thus emblematic of the evil that is contained in human souls and the evils of society at large. Foster also argues that ghosts and vampires and the like may not have to take literal forms - they can be used as a narrative vehicle to illustrate the phenomenon of a consuming spirit or vampiric personality.

An example that Foster expounds upon is the character of governess in Henry James' *The Turn of the Screw* (1898) who fantasizes that a ghost possesses her wards, and in her delusion smothers them with protectiveness. Here the motif of a ghost (which may or may not be real) can be read as a commentary on the psychological state of a mother figure as well as fatherly neglect. In another James novel, *Daisy Miller* (1878), the fate of young Daisy at the hands of her cold love interest, Winterbourne is a case of a vampiric personality manifestation. The story also indicates the stifling and consuming nature of a society that operates on rigid social customs. Foster concludes by pointing out how the vampiric, ghostly or spooky spectre has appeared throughout the ages, as during the naturalistic movement of the late nineteenth century down to the twentieth century works of writers such as Franz Kafka and D.H. Lawrence. The recurrence of this motif, according to Foster, is simply indicative of exploitation and selfishness in various guises and remains a literary convention that will continue to haunt us so long as we do wrong by our fellow men/women.

Analysis:

Foster's identification of the quest tale is an important recognition of a theme that pervades literary texts, but the significance of the 'journey' may go well beyond literature itself. The book's allusion to medieval quest imagery such as the knight and the Holy Grail is not the starting point for this subject - indeed quest is an older tradition that reaches back to the classical age. In her work, *The Idea of the Labyrinth: From Classical Antiquity to the Middle Ages*, Penelope Doob traces the historic roots and usage of the journey motif that has become a part of our collective consciousness.

Some of the earlier usages of the quest was related to matters of the Divine - often labyrinths or mazes would consist of twelve concentric circles, alluding to the planetary movements or structure. Critics have also analyzed the quest as man's recognition of the confusion and disorder that often dominates the world and human life, but which is ultimately part of a Divine system of perfection and order as suggested by the workings of Nature. The quest then becomes a symbol of the universal endeavor to find the right path, the clear road or meaning. As a long-standing tradition, it also points to an impulse that is at the basic unit of what it means to be human.

Doob's book is also illuminative in highlighting the different forms that a quest tale can take. The author distinguishes for instance between the quest that is a physical journey, and one that is intellectual. Foster doesn't quite reflect on how the road or journey need not be an explicitly physical one; the paths that our thoughts, intellectualism, emotions and beliefs take can be as significant in implications as a physical quest. Intellectual labyrinth, then, is also a feature of the quest that readers would do well to keep in mind. Doob's research doesn't merely focus on literature: it consults manuscripts, illustrations, carvings and drawings in Church buildings, to name a few. What this suggests is that the quest is as much a cultural feature as it is a literary one - it's centrality over the ages in human lives makes its appearance in literary texts all the more telling.

Another equally significant literary and cultural theme is food - the subject of Foster's second chapter ("Acts of Communion"). While Foster is right in stressing the implications of a meal scene and the communal bonds it forms, according to writer Victoria Best, his analysis doesn't quite go far enough. Best argues for instance how acts of communion or shared meals differ from culture to culture, and thus how implications vary as well. Thus in a text that is centered around French society, a meal scene vividly described is an indication not just of communion between the eating members, but also of the French attitude towards food which is regarded almost as a work of art. Whereas it involves aesthetics in French society, food in British literature might be more significant in drawing family and friends together because of the war-time rationing and scarcity. In other words, according to Best, there are "different understandings of what constituted communion in the first place."

A discussion on vampires and ghosts, and perhaps other supernatural elements might be remiss without a consideration of Gothic literature. This genre has its own implications altogether, but some are contained in the features that Foster chooses specifically to focus on, that is, vampirism. Foster rightly argues that the vampire is a symbol for human exploitation, sexuality, selfishness amongst other ills, but it is also seen as a more extreme "perversion" of reality and normality. Paradoxes such as "living dead" and "heroic antagonist" associated with literary vampires are indicative of deeper impulses within the human psyche for the dark, the abnormal, and the perverse.

In *A Parasitic Perspective: Romantic Participation and Polidori's The Vampyre*, Scholar J.P Telotte traces the first appearance of the vampire in literature, describing him as "a fundamental perversion of normal human participation in the world" (10). Telotte sees the vampire as a reflection of society's perception of the world and man's place in this world. Efforts to fight the vampire in a story, then, can be symbolic of efforts to fight against perversion and uphold the ideal form of living or participating in this world.

Yet another interesting perspective is offered by a scholar tracing the development of the ghost story in *The Blood is the Life* who argues how "...the ghost story became a vehicle not only for entertainment but also for expression for the uneasy fluctuations of the belief on the part of the cognitive minority no longer content with the Christian supernatural yet appalled by the new scientism whose presuppositions they sought to reject or soften." Thus in several ways the ghost is also - even indirectly - a symbol of struggles between religion and practicality, faith and reason. A reader or student of literature is not expected to know or adopt the viewpoints put forward by the scholars, but understanding the various dimensions of a literary trope such as vampire or ghost can add meaning as well as shed some light on the historic/social conditions in which the text was set.

How to Read Literature Like a Professor Chapters 4-6 Summary and Analysis

Summary:

In chapter four Foster introduces poetry, specifically the sonnet form, which he chooses for its prevalence, its versatility, and ease in identification. The sonnet, in other words, is the mode of poetry most likely to be encountered by a literature student, and knowledge of its structure, use and effect is thus quite essential. Foster describes the square geometry of the sonnet as its most distinguishing feature - sonnets are fourteen lines long and written in iambic pentameter which is a regular rhythm comprising of stressed and unstressed syllables. Usually lines in the poetry will have eight to ten syllables and such consistency combined with the standard 14-line length yields a square verse. Although Foster concedes that poems can and should be read for enjoyment without an in-depth understanding of its structural features, he also points out that much of the 'magic' or effect of the poetry is conveyed through its organization.

The writer states that the sonnet can be thought of as having two units of meaning that are related but with a certain shift between them. The sonnet thus breaks into two parts, the first comprising of eight lines and the second of six lines (given the ubiquitous use of the sonnet since the 1500s, many variations of this division exist, but the majority can be said to follow the aforementioned form). To illustrate these features and the implications they have on the content, Foster analyzes Christina Rossett's 'An Echo from Willow-Wood' (ca. 1870). The first eight lines (the octave) are written in a pattern that stresses the basic concept of the potential for separation of two lovers whilst the last six (the sestet) marks the transition in meaning and actualizes the possibility of separation into a reality. Foster concludes by pointing out how Rossetti manages to pack a lot of meaning relating to complex human feelings in a highly dense and constrained form. The vessel of the poem - the sonnet form - thus becomes part of the poem's meaning.

Chapter five discusses the recurrence of familiar figures, archetypes and images in literary works. This follows the familiar idea that literature builds upon other literature and stories grow out of other stories. Foster discusses this point primarily by analyzing Tim O'Brien's *Going After Cacciato* (1978). He demonstrates ways in which various events and parts of the story are inspired by other stories read by the author, stored in memory or personally experienced. An example is the character of Sarkin Aung Wan, the protagonist's love interest, who recalls the figure of Sacajawea. The act of drawing upon other texts is a largely conscious and purposeful process by the writer and indicative of the creative process at large. One of the reasons why such borrowing occurs is because in actuality there is only one story -

that of the human experience. Writing merely seeks to represent and comment upon this in various guises.

Critics often refer to the links between literary works and texts as 'intertextuality'. According to Foster, when a reader can recognize patterns and/or similarities within a text then the reading experience is significantly improved and the multiple layers of meaning revealed. Intertextuality can also be used to challenge reader expectations; Foster describes how author Angela Carter in her novel *Wise Children* (1992) uses characters that are highly nostalgic of Shakespearean characters, but as the novel progresses, behave in ways that challenge traditional Shakespeare plotlines. The author draws on earlier texts but also uses this as a literary strategy to affect the reading experience and expectation.

Understanding intertextuality and how to use it in analysis of literature is a very useful skill to have, and one that is steadily developed over time through practice, extensive reading, and knowing what one should be looking for. While this isn't crucial to enjoy a work of literature, it nonetheless allows for a deeper understanding of how complex and rich a story can be.

In chapter 6 Foster extends the discussion on intertextuality to focus exclusively on Shakespeare and the Shakespearean tradition. Knowledge of Shakespearean works is important because of their ubiquity - literary texts and indeed other art forms including film, poetry and of course theater have drawn inspiration from, or else directly borrowed storylines, characters, and dialogue from these Old English plays. Our familiarity with phrases such as " All the world's a stage / And all the men and women merely players," "And flights of angels sing thee to thy rest," and "The quality of mercy is not strained, It droppeth as the gentle rain from Heaven" to mention only a few, indicate the prevalence of Shakespeare not only in literary circles but popular culture as well. Foster goes on to argue that such ubiquity is significant and can be explained in part by the value that a Shakespearean reference adds to a literary work.

Shakespeare bestows a certain authority and credibility to the writer's work in part because of it is so universally recognizable. Foster also asserts that Shakespeare provides a platform for writers to develop, exchange and bounce ideas. A reference to a popular figure such as the tragic hero Hamlet can be far more effective in conveying a character's internal struggle or personality than an entire passage of description devoted to this task. Moreover, the engagement and dialogue that texts in each era have with Shakespearean works are telling indicators of features of that particular period - whether writers model their works after Shakespearean plays or characters, or else challenge them, ultimately inform us of how perceptions and social conditions have evolved over time. As readers, we participate in this creation of meaning and utilize our imagination that is integral to this creation process.

Analysis:

When it comes to poetry, the appearance or structure of the writing is perhaps as significant as the story it contains which is why Foster is write to highlight the sonnet

How to Read Literature Like a Professor Chapters 4-6 Summary and form. Even modern poetry, which hopes to break away from conventions and is written in a free-style with seemingly no conventions, is significant in itself for what it indicates of rejecting tradition, setting new trends etc. Another feature of the sonnet that deserves attention is the beat or sound conveyed through its iambic structure or rhythm. When reading a poem, it is best to read aloud and notice if the manner in which the syllables are sounded relate to the meaning of the words - in a somber poem perhaps, the stressed syllables would relate to heavier and shorter words whilst in a more ironic or satirical poem, longer words, broken up into several syllables each indicating its own meaning might be found.

Closely related to the subject of sonnets is Shakespeare, yet another reason for recalling his influence on literary conventions as Foster describes. Although the sonnet predates this Elizabethan writer, scholars have focused exclusively on the Shakespearean sonnet to point out ways in which this form developed further. Some suggest that the sonnet as we know it today was a modern theme which Shakespeare paved the way for - earlier it was restricted in the form it could take on, and the themes it could discuss.

With Shakespeare's lively language and adherence to the structure of the sonnet allowed the stories/dialogue/text to take on a greater intensity. In other words, Shakespearean sonnets allowed for economy of words whilst maximizing meaning. Borris Ford in *The Age of Shakespeare* states how the Shakespearean sonnet "encouraged the association of compression with depth of content and variety of emotional response to a degree unparalleled in English". Thus, when reading a sonnet, it is wise to keep in mind that there may be several layers of meaning embedded in the text than might otherwise seem on a first reading.

Foster's argument that literature often contains echoes from previous or other works is not a new idea - as the author himself points out, writers before him have described how stories are built upon other stories. There are debates however, over the extent to which one must be familiarized or learn to identify intertextuality when reading a book. Not all professors, in their analysis of texts, focus on external influences (although resonance to certain archetypes or features commonly features in studies). For a reader, or even student of literature, it is even more unclear whether one should be trained in seeing these resonances or recurring imagery. Certainly they are not, as the author himself concedes, critical to enjoying the subject. But such features need not even guide analysis at a high school or college level.

Foster's book is directed towards students of literature and its attempts to be accessible and easy to read suggests that a more professional audience (such as graduate students) is not the target. In light of this, then, one does well to consider requirements of a college level English course where students are normally expected to write a paper with their own, individual thesis and analysis. This analysis then rests largely upon the features of the text that are of interest to the student him/herself and certainly doesn't require a working familiarity of external influences. Often students are expected to analyze the story for itself, rather than in more generic ways that speak of the tradition/conventions of literature as a whole.

In assessing a literary convention, one must always ask: "What are the implications of this convention to the story/text I am reading?" So too is the case with the literary feature of Shakespearean influence. Towards the end of the discussion Foster points out that authors may include references to the Bard in order to lend authority to the text, to make it sound more significant perhaps or more complex. This is certainly true, and furthermore, references to earlier works can also be seen as manifestations of the human impulse for nostalgia and connection.

Our interest in the past and in the lives of those gone before us is in some ways an attempt to seek a connection with fellow persons who may not share the same time or context as us, but who nonetheless share in the human experience of participating. Whether the text recalls a Shakespearean element, or characters in the text themselves, such recollection can be broadly viewed as an understanding that we are not so very different from our predecessors, nor are the themes, feelings and events that guide our lives very unique.

How to Read Literature Like a Professor Chapters 7 - 9 Summary and Analysis

Summary:

The theme of intertextuality continues on in chapter 7 where the writer discusses the literary significance and influence of the Bible. Foster points out how pervasive scriptural influence and reference has been, a fact that might be accounted for by the Bible's nonsectarian nature. Those outside of the Judeo-Christian world can also recognize Biblical imagery or quotation because of how popular scriptural allusions are. Although Foster opens the discussion through an analysis of Toni Morrison's *Beloved* (1987) and James Joyce' *Araby* (1914), much of what we know about Biblical use in literature has come from writers and poets before mid-twentieth century that were well instructed in religion. Classics such as *Beowulf*, *Paradise Lost*, and *The Canterbury Tales* all draw heavily upon religious and scriptural themes and motifs.

Contemporary writers possess a reasonable understanding of the Biblical tradition as well - many modern poets who produced spiritual poetry used biblical language and imagery. These include T.S. Eliot, Adrienne Rich, Geoffrey Hill, and Allen Ginsberg, all of who wrote on biblical subjects as diverse as redemption, disciples, Lenten consciousness and the Day of Atonement. However religious references need not be paying homage to the faith or tradition - modern and postmodern texts often draw upon biblical sources in an ironic mode, emphasizing differences and challenges rather than similarities and continuity of belief/ideas.

A classic example would be Salman Rushdie's *Satanic Verses* (1988). Although the work was directed towards the Islamic tradition, the concept of challenging an ancient, well known religious tradition through literary irony applies just as much. Foster also identifies key literary areas where the Bible asserts itself, each carrying its own significance. These include general aspects such as theme, archetypes, plot, but also more specific features of the text such as titles, situations and quotations, and names (Jacob, Rebecca, Mary, Joseph). Foster clarifies that it isn't necessary to be a Bible scholar in order to identify these parallels, but the reader can detect allusions to older/bigger texts by noting moments in the text that seem to indicate something outside the scope of the story or poem. The author terms this the 'resonance test,' and to illustrate its use references his experience of James Baldwin's story "Sonny Blues" (1957). A particular phrase in the story, "like the very cup of trembling" was quite resonant - and while Foster didn't attempt to learn its significance during initial readings, he eventually discovered that the description came from Isaiah 51:17.

Although this piece of knowledge isn't necessary to enjoy or even appreciate the work's ingenuity, the biblical dimension adds a certain depth to the seemingly simple story of Sonny and his brother. The story becomes reminiscent of distant antecedents, timeless myths and archetypes.

In chapter eight Foster outlines yet another literary source for allusion but one that is likely to be understood by a much wider audience - children's literature. While references to Shakespeare and the Bible can make the text in question seem more highbrow or complex, allusions to tales as familiar as *Alice in Wonderland, Treasure Island,* and fairy tales enable the story to be more accessible and relatable. In much the same way that writers draw on the well established works of Shakespeare to challenge reader's expectations of what will follow, so too do writers drawing on children's tales subvert original plotlines and character profiles to retell the story. Angela Carter series of stories in *The Bloody Chamber* (1979) challenge sexist underpinnings in traditional fairytales and instead present feminist revisions of these works.

Foster also points out that one of the effects of borrowing from earlier works of literature is irony that can appear in various guises. If a student can detect fairytale references (or others) then he/she should also be aware of the text taking on an ironic mode. Foster also makes a subtle point about what readers expect and want from a tale - novelty but familiarity too. If a text can achieve the harmony of providing a story that is unique but also reminiscent of tales, images, themes encountered from other texts, then, the writer argues, a certain depth and resonance is added to the text and to the reader's experience of it.

Foster seals the discussion on intertextuality by expounding upon yet another important literary influence - that of Greek mythology - in chapter 9. Although 'myth' is widely misunderstood as referring to a story or narration that is untrue, Foster uses the term to refer to the phenomenon of sustained story and symbol. A mythological story is thus relevant to the student of literature insofar as it influences and shapes a particular text or poem. Myths are especially significant in representing the story of a particular community a time, yet a story that contains universal elements in that it allows us unique ways to explain and ultimately read ourselves. Foster focuses particularly on the lasting influence of Greek mythology on the European and Euro-American cultures, an influence so strong that it has seeped into popular consciousness through daily references such as city or high school names (e.g. Troy, Athens, Remus).

Foster also explains that the sustained use and prevalence of mythological stories even in modern texts (such as parallels between the story of Crete and Daedalus and Toni Morrison's 'Song of Solomon') can be explained by the universality and reliability of themes - while particular plotlines might not be relevant in present contexts, human emotions such as wrath, neglect, loyalty and honor are still very much at play. Again, writers who wish to convey an ironic effect may overturn the similarities, an effect that is achieved largely because of how recognizable these myths are in popular consciousness.

Analysis:

The analysis in the last section regarding Shakespeare and intertextuality is equally true of allusions to the Bible and Greek mythology. Both fall under the category of myth (a long standing historic body of story) and as such, both can be seen as expressions of human nostalgia. Consequently, such references that suggest continuity in the human trajectory can help reveal something of our own existence and lives.

In the case of the Bible, specifically, this recollection and attempt to draw in the past to the present has implications other than nostalgia because of the very religious nature of this text. In other words, a biblical reference might be an affirmation of the messages and lessons brought down by the Prophets and sages of old. It can also be a subtle acknowledgement of the Divine and the variety of ways in which images, stories, and characters are used are indicative of how religion is constantly negotiated and reworked not just by communities and periods but also by individuals and characters.

The relationship between the Bible and literature, however, is not as linear as Foster's discussion might suggest. The author talks about the variety of ways in which Biblical imagery or words manifest themselves in literature, and while this influence certainly exists, as research in Biblical studies and related fields suggest, literature is often itself a commentary on the Bible, and a tool of analysis. Both traditions then inform each other, a symbiotic relationship that is perhaps less evident in other sets of mythological works. What this means for the student is to recognize that Biblical allusions, in addition to lending authority to the text/story (if used un-ironically) are just as indicative of the English-speaking world's understanding, shaping, and interpretation of the religious tradition (Jeffrey, 1992).

The other tradition identified by Foster as featuring in many literary texts, Fairytales, also merits consideration of what it can say/tell us about the story. Foster points out that writers may employ children's stories to reach out to a wider audience - but they may also be paying tribute to the adage that wisdom is often contained in the simple or in children. Fairytales exert an influence not merely because they have been sustained as a body of literature, or because they are easy to understand, but also because they carry a strong appeal of imparting valuable lessons and knowledge despite their seemingly childish or simplistic nature. Authors like Tim O'Brien who reference children's stories writers such as Lewis Carroll seem to be paying tribute to this very fact.

Fairytales also represent a kind of literary nostalgia, but one that is more personal and individual. References to children's literature may point to the child in each and every one of us - and the universal desire to return to a time of innocence and simplicity (although of course not every childhood is a a carefree one). Nonetheless, one of the possibilities that children's literature or fairytale references suggest is underscoring the naïveté, childlike inexperience that is always present in us no matter our age, because of the very fallibility of human nature. Thus a text that contains such allusions might be suggesting that the character - or society - for all its developments, still retains and manifests its original state of childishness. Writers can employ this in various ways - to convey a positive, endearing aspect of a character/society, or to comment upon its naive foolishness/blindness.

How to Read Literature Like a Professor 10 - 12 and Interlude Summary and Analysis

Summary:

Chapter 10 analyzes the significance that weather carries in a story. Certain qualities are so closely associated with particular forces of nature, such as the concept of rebirth with spring, or purification through rain, that descriptions of the environment often have implicit undertones and meaning which a student should look out for. Focusing on one of the most common literary weather symbol - rain - Foster explains how this phenomenon is saturated with meaning thanks in part to the religious traditions of old - the Judeo-Christian-Islamic have repeated references to rain as a cleansing/purifier and Divine blessing in their texts and oral narrations.

Rain and its by-product, flood, are also a force to be reckoned with (as in Noah's experience) but for all its awesome and destructive nature, usually also signals a fresh start. Other meanings associated with rain include mystery and foreboding ("It was a dark and stormy evening"), unification (it discriminates against no one) and even misery. Rain is also the principle component of spring ("April showers") and spring in turn is the season of renewal and hope. Modernist writers such as Eliot often subvert these traditional perceptions through their use of irony, playing against our cultural expectations in a deliberate way, "April is the cruellest month."

Another important symbol closely linked with rain is rainbows, a motif that not only carries messages of optimism but also signals biblical discourse, a kind of interaction between God, the world and human. Snow, another variant of rain, is equally varied in meaning and symbolism. It is also a unifier, and can be clean, purifying, stark, cold, severe, a warm or else suffocating blanket.

In the Interlude, Foster takes a break from his analysis of literary conventions to consider the question of writer intent - do authors really intend their work to be so allusive or symbolic in meaning? The writer's short answer is yes, although he clarifies that no one really knows for certain. Many modernist writers such as James Joyce and T.S. Eliot deliberately intended every effect and meaning in their writing, and are thus referred to as the "Intentionalists." It is important to note, moreover, that several of these writers and their contemporaries were well versed with the classics, the ancient religious texts, and the series of works that make up the literary canon. Pre-modern writers too were largely well instructed in Latin or Greek, and extensive classical poetry and prose including Dante and Shakespeare. Readers were also expected to have considerable training in the literary tradition.

Foster reminds us of how long literary composition can take - a chapter can often involve weeks of deliberation and lateral thinking, a quality that almost makes inevitable references to outside texts, Biblical/classical parallels, familiar symbolism and imagery and other details that make a work of literature so pregnant with meaning.

In chapter 11 Foster described how violence in literature goes beyond the literal description of a physical tussle. One of the literary examples the writer chooses to draw upon is Robert Frost's "Out, Out - " (1916) which is an overtly violent poem - it discusses how a momentary lapse of attention causes a hand to be lost to a buzz saw. Yet the poem is not simply about the dangerous nature of farm machinery, instead, it can be seen as commentary upon the often violent relationship humans have with the universe, the unexpectedness yet inevitability of death, and the smallness of our lives. Foster distinguishes then between two categories of violence in literature - the specific injury causes by characters on themselves or others, and the narrative violence that causes harm in general. The latter category is what comes to affect plot and thematic development, and characters' fate.

Foster also argues that violence which carries deeper implications is more evocative than violence that just is - mystery novels for instance seldom elicit much emotion from readers with regards to incidents of death or attack because these serve merely as tools for the main concerns of solving a problem, answering a riddle/question, finding the culprits etc. In other genres however, a death is not merely an incident or tool, but an event pregnant with meaning - a ominous portend, a character's desperation, an indicator of a community or race's experience. In Toni Morrison's *Beloved* for instance, Sethe's act of killing her daughter is a commentary on the deep struggles and anguish faced by a race at a particular moment in the past.

Even violence without agency, that is, what doesn't happen between character to character, is often do deliberately plotted and crafted by the writer that is usually points to deeper meanings. The student's task is to always ask what the misfortune represents thematically, psychologically, socially, historically, spiritually and even politically. An act of violence will rarely encompass all the above considerations, but it will possibly contain enough layers of meaning to merit a deeper read.

In chapter 12 Foster articulates the formal conventions governing symbols. His main thesis is emphasizing the complex nature of a symbol in that they rarely have a single meaning. Literary devices that do have a clear, one-cut interpretation are referred to as "allegories" where one thing stands for another. In John Bunyan's *The Pilgrim Progress,* for instance, the protagonist, Christian, encounters characters such as Evangelist, Giant Despair, and Faithful. The names of the characters are clear in indicating the qualities possessed by these figures, and in turn, the qualities encountered by a human (or pilgrim) during his journey/life. The figurative construct has a specific meaning and message that it hopes to convey.

This is not the case with symbols, however. In E.M. Forster's *A Passage to India,* caves take on various meanings because they are viewed in different ways by the characters in the novel itself. They are mysterious and strangely alluring for all, but also oppressive for one, and a means of accessing the deepest levels of consciousness for another. The caves even stand in as symbolic indicators of the ills of colonialism and its hypocrisy. One of the effects of the ambiguity surrounding symbols is that it often means what we - the readers - understand it to mean. Foster uses the discussion on symbolism to point out how, as readers, we bring in a certain background and perspective that inevitably influences the reception of the literary text in question and results in an individuality that makes the reading experience so unique - and the meaning of the text so complex.

Symbols are further complicated by the fact that they are used in different ways by different writers; the river, for instance, is used by Eliot in "The Wasteland" to be a symbol of effects of a World War, of the disintegration of Western civilization and modern life, whereas in Mark Twain's *The Adventures of Huckleberry Finn* the river is both danger and safety, a route to freedom but also a means of peril and adventure. Foster also cautions against thinking that only objects or images can be symbols, actions and events can be equally symbolic as well.

To navigate the complex seas of symbolism, Foster recommends focusing on our instinctual, affective response to literature that can shed light on what we understand the symbol to mean. However we also can't ascribe meaning where there isn't any - our creative imagination has to work with the imagination of the writer. The best dialogues are ones that take place on account of our having exercised our symbolic imagination, when we learn to note possible meanings or ideas during our readings that the symbol in question might indicate, contextualize the text and author, and of course, listen to our feelings.

Analysis:

For deeper understanding of the importance of weather in literary texts, one might consult writer J.E. Cirlot who, in his *A Dictionary of Symbols*, notes how the interplay between climate and character psychology is one of the most frequently recurring tropes in literature. He says,

"The relationship between a state of mind and a given climate, as expressed by the interlay between space, situation, the elements and temperature, as well as level-symbolism, is one of the most frequent of all analogies in literature. The universal value of pairs of opposites, such as high/low, dry/wet, clear/dark, is demonstrated in their continued use not only in physical and material but also in psychological, intellectual and spiritual matters."

Cirlot's analysis then, also looks at weather as a psychological tool that can help a reader gain insight into the character(s)' state of mind. This is not always the case of course; when surroundings are completely distinct from inner thoughts and emotions then the writer is employing weather in an ironic way. At the same time, weather can itself affect thoughts or psychology - Dickens' characters, particularly the somber or more afflicted ones, can be seen as extensions of dark, cloudy London.

It is perhaps impossible to reach a conclusion on the question of writer's intent without taking a position with one literary school of thought over another - Foster's assertion that writers do intend the layers of meaning in their work makes the latter seem like Intentionalists and the literary text a deliberately crafted production. This is not always the case however, as Foster himself acknowledges - and while he does suggest that the time it takes to write a book/poem or the "amnesia" that the writer has to practice contributes to the layers of meaning he focuses less or at least does not explicitly refer to influences that the writer may not be aware of him/herself.

Writers, in other words, can be affected subconsciously by certain prevailing social or historic trends which make their way into their worked even if the author isn't interested in writing about them. At times this influence may be entirely unconscious - our categorization of movements of literature as 'modern' or 'postmodern' or 'Victorian' often occur when sufficient time has passed for scholars of literature to look back and judge a certain period or century from a more 'objective' viewpoint. Consequently, the reader would do well to keep in mind that literary classifications are often fluid terms in and of themselves, and far from rigid, completely authentic, categories.

Foster's discussion of the significance of violence as a literary convention undoubtedly highlights a frequent element of literature; but other possibilities and forms of violence might exist that have gone unexplored. In contemplating violence the shrewd reader would realize that not all violence has to be explicitly identified in the text or described in physical terms - in the introduction to *The Violence of Representation,* authors Nancy Armstrong and Leonard Tennenhouse identify violence as the suppression of differences or as the assertion of one authority/power over another. Thus, for instance, in Jane Eyre's repression by her aunt and other figures although never physical, is nonetheless analyzed as a form of violence. The theme of violence is also closely associated with politics - violence between sexes or classes or even within family can have political undertones. Politics, it should be noted, doesn't necessarily have to relate to government but is often also used to refer to competing ideologies.

How to Read Literature Like a Professor Chapters 13 - 15 Summary and Analysis

Summary:

Often when a story or its characters or plot resonate with us, it is because some element of the text is representative of conditions or individuals in our society and world. More often than not such representativeness carries political implications as well - leading Foster to highlight the importance of understanding the political undertones of a literary piece. Foster distinguishes between overtly political writing which includes literature whose main intent is to influence the prevailing political thought/ideology and "political" writing that is more subtle and perhaps more effective. Political writing offers a perspective into the realities of the world and in doing so touches upon themes and problems that are collectively shared and thus relatable. Edgar Allen Poe for instance provides a criticism of the European class system and its elitism in his poems "The Masque of the Red Death" and "The Fall of the House of Usher." Both poems look at the conditions and practices of the nobility, and emerge as commentary upon the systems of monarchy and aristocracy.

Political undertones can also be found in seemingly apolitical texts such as Rip Van Winkle. Because political considerations are closely entwined with social, economic, historic and cultural issues, it is unsurprising that many texts can be said to be political in nature. Consequently, Foster argues that knowing something about the political and social context in which the writer was writing is significant for it can add a dimension to the text which readers, in their own unique political settings, might not have realized.

In chapter 14 Foster analyzes the Christian trope found in works of European and American literature. The dominance of cultural influences brought by early European settlers has meant that Christian values have been deeply woven in our social fabric, the consequent of which is that we live in a Christian culture. This influence can be ascertained in works of literature as well, in fact, texts draw so heavily upon this religious tradition that knowledge of the Old and New Testaments is quite essential. It is important to note that the values that appear in a text, while technically "Christian," need not take on a religious role but are more significant in revealing something about the character, plot, or theme of the story.

One of the more frequent Biblical archetypes used in literature is the figure of Christ, and Frost recommends familiarizing oneself with certain features of his character that appear in various guises in literary texts. These include qualities such as self-sacrificing, closeness with children, loaves, fish, water and wine, thirty-three years of age, crucifixion, and so forth. While some literary figures closely resemble Christ

(Ernest Hemingway's *The Old Man and the Sea* is replete with Christian imagery) others are more ambiguous, and indeed do not even have to embody the characteristic features of being male, Christian, or even good (in the latter's case, the parallel to Christ figure becomes an irony). Allusions to Christ can have various effects, from emphasizing the character's sacrifice by relating it to Divine sacrifice, ushering notions or hope/redemption/miracle or even portraying the character as much smaller by highlight the discrepancy between him/her and the figure of Christ.

Although flight is not a skill humans can lay claim to, our fascination with flying has remained with us to this day. It is unsurprising, then, that flight should feature so prominently in literature, and what is perhaps more pertinent is the literary implications it carries. Writers from the time of Greek mythology - and possibly well before - have ascribed various meanings and symbolic significance to descriptions of flight. Flying can represent freedom, escape, exuberance, largeness of spirit, even love, but if gone wrong it can also symbolize downfall (in the metaphoric and literal sense), danger, and helplessness. For the most part, however, flight according to Foster represents freedom and the motif is found and manipulated in various ways in different literary works.

Flight doesn't only have to appear in the literal sense, however: figurative flights are just as laden with meaning. In *A Portrait of the Artist as a Young Man*, James Joyce presents his protagonist as someone who feels trapped by the social, religious, political and personal constraints and the struggle to throw off these fetters, so to speak, conveys a distinct sense of metaphorical flight that is further compounded by the images of birds, feathers and flying in the second half of the novel. Often, flight is also a stand-in for a freeing of the spirit or soul into realms that reach our furthest imaginations. Flying, then, opens a host of possibilities, for the character and text in question, as well as for the analytical reader.

Analysis:

The featuring of Christ in literature is a complex literary convention, one that has been in use for centuries. Readers can perhaps get a sense of how heavy and lasting this feature is when we consider Rosemary Woolf's research. Woolf draws parallels between the knight figure and Christ, arguing how the latter was represented in medieval culture (and perhaps even before) as the knight who embarks on the quest. This is certainly a fresh way to consider the importance of the journey and knight motif that Foster presents in the first chapter. More importantly, it underscores how pervasive Christ has been in literature, in forms that are perhaps not easily recognizable. This affirms Foster's argument, then, that literature that contains Christ symbolism may not be completely true to the persona that emerges in religious texts or scripture, which is to say, not all characteristics of Christ may be outlined. Woolf's studies can also help us see how perhaps many literary conventions - including but not limited to the quest/knight motif - trace their origins to Christianity.

Of course the relationship is never so simple - Christianity or its perceptions may in turn be informed by culture including literature. One should also note that there is a difference between overtly religious literature and literature that contains religious references - the latter is what Foster is referring to when discussing the Christ trope. The subtle difference between the two can be assessed by noticing for what purposes the character which resembles Christ is used - religious literature is likely to explicitly identify the cause as one of salvation or Divine intervention whereas this is not the central theme or indeed purpose of other literary texts. Robert Detweiler who studies the Christ trope in American Fiction makes an interesting argument, saying "Perhaps the creation of the Christ figure has to remain the task of the secular writer, for the religious novelist who attempts to work with it finds himself caught in an uneasy liaison: the doctrinal Jesus he propagandizes and the symbolic Christ he tries to fashion invariably get in the way of each other, so that eventually both the art and the all-important message of his story suffer." While ultimate conclusions on the 'effectiveness' of the Christ persona - and even whether the question of effectiveness matters at all - rests with the reader, it is nonetheless interesting to consider how Christ fares in secular literature such as that which Foster analyzes.

Foster's analysis of flight echoes conclusions drawn by Swiss psychologist Carl Jung who identifies flying as symbolic of freedom, escape, attempts for liberation and so forth, pointing to the almost universal meaning that we attach with such actions. Foster discusses how flying can appear in various forms, through imagery, plot, themes and so forth but it is also helpful to consider other symbols that represent flight - and which carry more or less the same meaning as flying itself. These objects or symbols include the sky, birds, feather, wind, clouds and shooting stars to mention a few. Flying and its symbolism, then, can be communicated through indirect means and doesn't necessarily involve characters who dream of flying, or who fly themselves.

An important theme related to flying is also what it reveals about the human attraction to the unknown. Flying into the skies or heavens, in others words to realms that we are unfamiliar with and which are "foreign" suggests a basic human curiosity of what lies beyond the world we know as well as the tendency to seek out new territory. It is an example of man's consistent efforts to pursue knowledge, to assert himself or his presence in various spheres of life. In many ways flying is like traveling - but perhaps with more spiritual or metaphysical implications because of the otherworldly quality of the place of destination. An interesting assignment for literary students would be to compare the literary symbolism of ocean/sea journeys, land travels, and aerial flights.

Flight has also been a prominent trope in African-American literature and it is worth considering perspectives of scholars in this field because their analysis differs from Foster's and indeed from the common interpretations of flying. Scholars such as Guy Wilentz focus on folk legends of flight and resistance to argue that there are historic-culture specific symbolism associated with flying. In other words, different communities have varied understandings and interpretations of flight. For the African-American community, myths and traditions of flight have been specific to the escape/freedom from the shackles of slavery. This takes on even more complexity when we note that authors use 'slavery' in various ways in their works- it can be used to mean the actual physical ordeal that a community experiences, or even to mental slavery to self-perceptions/thoughts and/or to society's perspectives and judgment.

How to Read Literature Like a Professor Chapters 13 - 15 Summary and

How to Read Literature Like a Professor Chapters 16 - 20 Summary and Analysis

Summary:

Chapters 16 and 17 discuss sexual implications in literature. In chapter 16 Foster points out how Freudian theory has greatly influenced our capacity to uncover and realize the sexual potential of the subconscious, and more specifically, how this manifests itself in literature. The telling characteristic of such Freudian analysis is that reference to sexual behavior or character is rarely explicitly outlined - rather, it is contained within text that overtly seems to refer to something else. For this reason, settings (tall buildings are considered representative of male sexuality, rolling hills/landscapes indicative of female), objects (bowls, fires, lance) and even distinct activities (eating, fighting) can all be used by the writer to convey sexual notions.

The use of sexual imagery predates Freud, however, and as an example Freud offers the Grail legends of the knight whose quest is often one related to manhood and the coming together of the male and female (the 'Holy Grail' was traditionally an emblem of female sexuality). Often due to censorship laws, writers such as D.H Lawrence weren't allowed to explicitly include sexual scenes in their literature - yet they nonetheless managed to convey the impression they desired through other means, such as a dramatic exchange between characters or even wrestling in "Women in Love." But such forced disguise can often prove to be more effecting in that its coded nature allows for greater complexity and layers of meaning. This coupled with the reality of sex manifesting itself in various guises through our subconscious in turn affirms the effectiveness of an implicit rather than explicit sex scene.

In chapter 17 Foster continues the discussion on sexuality but points out that explicit references to sex actually mean everything but the act itself. He discusses how centuries of censorship that enabled black market texts on the subject have caused sex descriptions to become rather clichéd. Beyond this issue, however, a writer's deliberate attempt to describe a sex scene is usually indicative of various other themes relating to the character in question or the plot line. Henry Miller's works that are fairly replete with sexual imagery and acts are implicitly celebrating and claiming freedom from convention and restrictions. Lawrence Durrell's writing is often closely related to notions of sacrifice, psychological neediness, power, espionage and so forth. Female writers such as Angela Carter as also used sex as a means of subverting and commenting upon the dictates of a patriarchal world.

Another Christian motif that Foster believes to be prevalent in literature is that of drowning and baptism. A writer's decision to drown or else submerge and drench their characters can be revealing in many ways - and perhaps an even an extension of their own subconscious feelings and thoughts as Foster points out how a large number of writers met their fate (intentionally or unintentionally) in bodies of water. The case of a character being subsumed in water and re-emerging, either through rescue or fate, strongly suggests a rebirth of sorts - the type of symbolism contained in acts of baptism. Judith Guest's "Ordinary People" is an example of the use of such imagery where the protagonist Conrad struggles with the fact that he survives a drowning episode whilst his brother - who is stronger, more capable, and more loved - does not. Rebirth in this text suggests the pain associated with occupying a new life and position in the world, not least because it forces an entire shift in perspective on life, self, and the universe.

Often such symbolic experiences of baptism are also closely related to a character's growth or reformation, as is the case with Milkman in Toni Morrison's *Song of Solomon*. Foster also points out that while submersion and survival in water is heavy with Biblical imagery, Christianity is certainly not the only religion to lay claim to this practice or to emphasize the symbolic importance of water. Moreover, while the act can be spiritual, it doesn't always have to be so and may simply mark a new start or birth. Drowning, on the other hand, implies the opposite of what re-emergence from water might. It can be a symbol of personal or social failure, condemnation, guilt, racial commentary, and even plot complication.

Chapter 19 discusses the significance of setting in a literary work. Writers make a conscious decision to select a particular place or context, and it is thus important for the reader to consider the implications of the choice made. Geography, then, is an important feature of literary analysis for it shapes and influences the plotline, and even the characters behavior or personality. "The Old Man and the Sea" is situated in the Caribbean for obvious reasons, but is also proximal to Cuba, which in turn captures the complex American-Cuban history and relations. Foster describes literary geography as revealing something about humans inhabiting spaces as well as spaces inhabiting humans.

How a particular landscape or city it described can be an extension of social or personal psychology, attitude, politics, economics, or any other subjects that affect human lives. Geography can help develop a character or his/her fate, as is the case with Milkman Dead in Morrison's *Song of Solomon*. He leaves a fairly cosmopolitan home to travel to his family's home country and on the way, in the hills and hollows, discovers a sense of responsibility and undergoes a personal maturation. Often setting itself becomes character as in Tim O Brien's *Going After Cacciato,* where the land of Vietnam, unfamiliar territory for American soldiers, becomes a formidable and defensive opponent. Foster also states that trips to the South usually have dramatic (tragic or comic) implications for the character in question.

The writer also describes specific characteristics of symbolic importance relating to particular types of landscapes - prairies for instance conveys a vastness and beauty, mountains - featured prominently in the works of the Romantic poets - relay a certain majesty and sublimity. Hills carry their own significance least of which is the concept of higher and lower levels of land - the latter can contain swamps, people, darkness, fields, heat, unpleasantness, life whilst the former can suggest isolation, life, death, thin air, purity, clear views to name a few. The list is not exhaustive of course, and depending on the writer, qualities can be interchanged. The dynamism of human experience is often a factor of the setting we inhabit, and it is worth paying attention to the story or poem's location.

Chapter 20 looks at the meaning that seasons carry in literature. The four stages have been used in many ways - by Renaissance writers such as Shakespeare who have applied the progression of year and time and its varying nature to human life (the onset of age, for instance, is reminiscent of Autumn and Winter) and even by modernist authors such as Henry James who has used seasonal imagery for his characters' names (and personalities) (Daisy Miller and Frederic Winterbourne). Foster argues that the literary appeal of seasons lies in their almost universal understanding - spring is linked with childhood, youth, rebirth, hope, summer with romance, fulfillment, adulthood, autumn with decline and tiredness but also harvest (both personal and agricultural), and winter with old age, resentment, and death. Once this pattern is recognized, it is easy to discern it in its various guises and nuances in literary texts. Writers can choose to modify (or build on existing modifications) the use of seasons which makes seasonal symbolism all the more complex. Ironic modes may very well undermine traditional expectations with these stages, while straightforward uses would uphold the meanings discussed before. Since seasons have been with us in literature from the time of Greek mythology, and will continue to play a role in our consciousness of our universe, it is worth considering and identifying key patterns that have developed over the years.

Analysis:

Foster's reference to the Freudian movement can help identify the evolution of literature for the student. While it may very well be true that Freud identified objects/ images that had sexual implications rather than their overt, assumed meanings and offered a fresh perspective with which to read literature, it may also be the case that literature – specifically modernist and postmodernist movements from the time of Freud onward - were influenced by Freudian thought enough to consciously incorporate covert sexual references in their works. In other words, one is perhaps likely to find closer parallels to Freudian theories on symbols of our sexual subconscious in more contemporary works than in earlier texts where sexuality was represented according to that period and society's prevailing traditions. While sexuality can be represented in subtle and multiple ways, the reader should also be careful not to jump to conclusions or identify sexual acts where they may not exist. Analysis can be aided by researching the author's background, writing style with other works, and socio-historic environment.

Although Foster asserts that explicit descriptions of sex are actually symbolic of other, deeper meanings, it is also true that such deeper meanings can in fact suggest something of sex/sexuality itself. It can be a commentary on how sex is viewed or treated by the society presented in the text. In Vladimir Nabokov's *Lolita,* for instance, the protagonist's allusions to sex can reveal something of how this theme is treated and come to be understood in modern Western American culture – not pedophilia itself, but subtle allusions to the general conception of sex and sexuality. What makes the story, and the narrator so intriguing is how otherwise 'normal' the protagonist is – despite his aberration he is still a product of, and shaped by, the society in which he resides. It can be argued then that in some ways the narrator's perversity is an indictment of all of us –or at least of the society in which we participate.

The discussion on setting and environment in chapters 19 and 20 are closely related themes underscoring how literary conventions seldom operate in neatly distinguishable categories, for instance, themes of flight may arise because of the setting or location whilst Biblical as well as supernatural elements are closely tied. Setting and season – geographical location and the prevailing environment - are also similarly concurrent themes in a text and often an analysis of one necessitates, or leads to, an analysis of the other. Thus winter which can be symbolic of bitterness, difficulty, takes on different shades of complexity and meaning when it occurs in industrial London or mountainous highlands.

The setting of a work matters to reader as well because it can either be familiar or an insight into the foreign. Both have different and lasting impressions upon the reader's interaction with the text. Part of literature's appeal is that it transcends boundaries, and one of the most obvious, explicit ways in which it does this is to present settings and locations that are completely novel, but which nonetheless resonate because of common themes of the human experience. Great literature also has the capacity to express our homes and familiar societies in ways that ring true for us, causing us to relate not just to the work but also to our surroundings in deeper, complex, and perhaps more meaningful ways.

Just as setting informs the literary text, as Foster argues, so too can the text inform our relationship to our world. The task of the analytical student is to discern these resonances, to identify what features in the novel/poem elicit such responses with him/her so as to consider more deeply the literary conventions and tools the writer has employed in delivering this effect.

How to Read Literature Like a Professor Chapters Interlude and Chapters 21 - 24 Summary and Analysis

Summary:

In the interlude, Foster reaffirms the practice of intertextuality in literature. He addresses the question as to why and how works inevitably contain references to other texts. One of the reasons, discussed before, is the comfort of familiarity and recognition of elements seen during our prior reading - a quality that, if lacking, would make for quite an unnerving experience for readers. Foster also explains that writers, while they have to "forget" the materials they have read as they sit down to write, and incorporate the great tradition of literature and poetry unconsciously. Whether or not writers acknowledge these influences is another issue, but there is little doubt that the themes, stories, characters and images that have been retained in their subconscious guide their work. A distinguishing feature of intertextuality is also the concept of archetype which is a pattern that develops out of mythic original and which, because of its relatable nature and appeal, keeps recurring in works of literature, becoming stronger and more effective as they appear in increasing number of texts. Archetypes can include any component of stories, a quest, the knight character, a certain sacrifice etc. Foster concludes by stating that there has only really been one story that has been going on forever around us and which has enabled writers and readers to make use of literary structure, symbolic logic and shared knowledge.

In Chapter 21 Foster discusses the symbolic importance that physical marks or deformities take on in literature. Physical imperfections go beyond the body - they tell us something about the character's uniqueness or even of the prevailing social and political thought of the time. The Puritans and Shakespeare for instance wrote during a period where one's closeness or favor with God was manifested outwardly in the self or in their worldly lives. While scars or other shortcomings are by and large no longer considered as moral shortcomings or proof of divine displeasure, they nonetheless continue to mean various things in literature. The practice of marking characters goes back to the Folktales of the Slavs and persists to modern works of fiction such as Harry Potter. Individual markings each tell their own unique tale but all ultimately point to character differentiation.

The famed Greek mythological figure, Oedipus blinds himself - an impairment that suggests atonement, guilt, and grief - but he is in fact a marked man from the very beginning as his name suggests. Oedipus literally means wounded foot. His distinction as a public figure is well known through the narration of his fate and story. Frankenstein's menacing and damaged face is representative on some level of the darker side of science, forbidden quests, and a pact with the devil. Marked-ness need not imply something negative, as for instance in the case of the Hunchback of Notre-Dame, who has a beautiful soul but an unappealing exterior. Yet even his deformity can be a foreboding sign if we consider his eventual fate at the hands of death. Not all scars or disfigurements have to mean something, but if the writer chooses to single out a character due to a particular physical feature it is worth wondering why.

In chapter 22 Foster considers the implications of blindness as a literary feature. He notes that in introducing blindness, writers wish to emphasize other levels of sight or characteristics beyond the physical. A blind character requires a shift in perspective not only from his/her own position, but also requires change in behavior by others, even if these changes are subtle. Oedipus' physical blinding of his own self actually turns out to be an explicit manifestation of his inner blindness or inability to grasp the truth. Foster also states that when blindness and sight appear as themes in a work of literature, then related images and phrases increasingly emerge in the text. Most literary works deal with issues of darkness and light, seeing and blindness, even if there isn't a specifically blind character in the story. Those that do feature such figures possibly wish to cast even greater light on this subject, placing it in the forefront of their plot. In most such cases, Foster points out, writers tend to introduce the blind character fairly early on in the novel and readers who recognize this trope should keep a look out for related imagery and allusions.

Chapter 23 continues the discussion on health maladies by considering literary situations of heart diseases. Like blindness, which suggests meanings that go beyond the external, heart diseases usher in themes that guide the plot or the character. For Foster, heart disease is the most convenient and lyrical literary tool for writers largely because of the clear symbolism associated with it. As a symbolic repository of feeling and emotion, the heart says a great deal about the character - a heart of iron, heartbroken, a heart full to bursting - these are just some of the many heart references used to describe strong human emotions. Because this is a universally recognized meaning, writers are able to use heart ailments as indicative of their characters, their characters' humanity, or even a society's general ills. Heart disease can indicate bad love, cruelty, loneliness, pederasty, shock, cowardice, weakness of character and so forth. Heart ailments can be described even without recourse to an actual heart disease - Nathaniel Hawthorne's *The Man of Adamant* is about a misanthrope who secludes himself in a cave because he believes everyone else is a sinner. Yet because his limestone cave has drips of water that contains calcium, eventually the toxic liquid seems into his body causing his heart to turn into stone. The irony is clear, and indeed descriptions or references to physical ailments such as that of the heart make great use of irony in achieving some of their effects.

Foster's discussion on physical and health concerns continues in chapter 24 to encompass all illnesses in general. Health afflictions can be frustrating, even startling, in real life, but in literature we are less concerned with the bodily condition itself and more interested in what the disease tell us about the suffering character and the story at large (and perhaps even about the writer's intent). Diseases up until the twentieth century were by and large a mystery causing illnesses to take on a certain superstitious and fearful quality. Foster identifies four main governing principles for descriptions of illnesses in literature; firstly, illnesses are not given equal treatment, that is to say, some diseases tend to be favored in literature over others even if they occurred in great frequency primarily because of associated public perception (cholera, because of its rather unpleasant debilitating effects had a bad reputation whilst syphilis, evidence of sex beyond marriage, was taboo in its moral corruption implication); secondly, the illness used should be picturesque so that the physical alteration is dramatic in effect; third, they should be mysterious in origin, again for dramatic effect and to undermine expectations; and finally they should have strong symbolic or metaphoric interpretations (e.g. Tuberculosis, the wasting disease, could be used as a commentary on individual lives wasted away).

Foster points out that TB and cancer largely dominated the literary scene of illnesses throughout the nineteenth and early twentieth century whilst the plague has been a historic favorite. In our contemporary age, AIDS seems to have become a prominent feature of literary texts that contain reference to disease - its compelling allure can be attributed to the political and social commentary it offers and while it is particular to its time, it nonetheless conveys a universality of suffering, despair, self-control and loss that we can all relate to. For Foster, the ideal illness is one that is made up, or not clearly identified. Fevers fall under this category for their generic yet nonetheless health related implications - a writer is less restricted when the disease in unspecified for it doesn't require adherence to formalities such as its known causes, symptoms etc. The fever can represent the randomness of fate, the difficulty of life, the unpredictability of God's decree, and so forth. Admittedly in the modern age of medicine when diseases are more easily identified, the use of the generic fever is harder to pull off in literature.

Analysis:

References to intertextuality are interspersed throughout the book, and the chapter on intertextuality should be seen as a synthesis, or clearer exposition on this subject. However it is also important to note that "intertextuality" is not as separate or neat a category as the chapter might suggest - it is closely woven with another theme Foster discusses, that is, the idea that there is ultimately only one story in literature, which is about the human experience. How intertextuality functions also brings in other literary conventions such as archetypes, universal meanings, historic traditions or myth, and so forth. Rather than identifying it as a distinct component of literature, the reader would perhaps fare better in viewing intertextuality as woven into the complex web of literature, emerging often but in different ways.

Foster's discussion of physical marks rightly points out how writers differentiate certain characters from the rest. It is perhaps just as telling when there *are no* distinguishable marks on a prominent character or characters. A classic example would be the portrayal of identical twins in literature - at times one is distinguished from another by a tiny, seemingly innocuous mark such as a freckle on the finger, but when there are no such distinctions then internal characteristics or features become much more important. Similarly, characters described as perfectly fashioned should also be a cause for closer study. Foster largely discusses physical shortcomings in terms of dis-figuration but characters can also be marked by external elements such as tattoos or piercings.

In early Western culture the eyes were often prized as the most superior of sense organs and thus associated with notions of knowledge, man's superiority, and so forth. In light of this, then, blindness in literature takes on all the more significance. Maren Tova Linnett, who focuses on blindness and intimacy in early twentieth century literature, also looks at the ways in which writers used these themes over the centuries. She agrees with Foster's analysis of blindness symbolizing either lack of knowledge or profound insight, related to themes of light and darkness, but also states that perceptions of blindness have evolved over time. In pre-modern literature blindness couldn't lead to a completely fulfilling or happy life no matter its other benefits (the tradition of ocular-centrism - privileging of vision over other senses) but with changing beliefs, twentieth century and modernist literature have valued blindness over the ability to see. Blind characters are often presented as exuding a sense of calm or contentment, having been shielded from the anxieties that others are exposed to. More important is Linnett's argument that literary blindness is often associated with intimacy - where blind characters are better able to connect and communicate with people.

Foster's discussion of heart disease and illnesses in literature is another instance of how literature is a reflection of the human experience - for better and for worst. This also implies that the way in which such themes are presented in texts is affected in part by the prevailing socio-historic conditions. For instance, in the book *Victorian Poetry and the Culture of the Heart*, Kirstie Blair focuses on ways in which Victorian advances in medicine, and changing perceptions of the heart, affected the literary heart that poets and writers presented in their writing. For the Victorians the heart was seen as distinct and separate from mind and will, which accorded it a special place of significance. Blair argues that there was increasing suspicion on validity of feelings/emotions as well as rise in medical literature regarding the pathological heart, which led to a general sense of concern over its health. This general concern, experienced by poets and writers as well, ultimately made its way into Victorian poetry and text.

Blair's analysis offers a more practical perspective with which to read illnesses (heart and others) in literature. Whereas Foster focuses on the symbolism and possible implications of such themes, one can also engage more deeply with the text by understanding some of the broader factors that prevailed during the time the text was written. Knowing these conditions and the context in which the author wrote might enable readers to have a deeper insight into why the author chose the trope he did, and how it was likely to be received by the audience.

How to Read Literature Like a Professor Chapters 25 - 27 Summary and Analysis

Summary:

In Chapter 25, Foster stresses the importance of putting oneself in the character's shoes when reading the text. In other words, to appreciate the multi-layered nature of the work the reader has to approach the story from the perspective of the characters that he/she encounters. To give an example, Foster cites James Joyce's "The Dead," particularly the dinner scene where the family gathers for a holiday meal. So as to appreciate the true significance of the meal itself, the reader should consider it from the perspective of Aunts Kate and Julia for whom the meal is not only of religious significance, but a time of extravagance that enables them to hold on to a fading gentility and memories of the more luxurious comforts of the middle class.

As outsiders, we are less likely to grasp the reason for their anxiety over the gathering unless we understand how and why it is so important in their lives. Foster recommends maintaining a certain balance between adopting only the characters' eyes and sticking to our own. He suggests a reading perspective that considers the historical and social context of the story to understand the background against which the text was written. This involves, to a considerable degree, knowing or at least attempting to discern the author's viewpoint or intent. The writer acknowledges, however, that such an acceptance need not imply agreement with that period or culture's values - whilst knowledge of Greek paganism and values would inform our readings of mythology, it doesn't entail an endorsement of the prevailing customs and beliefs such as enslavement, execution, concubines etc. Another example is Shakespeare's *The Merchant of Venice*, which seems to contain anti-Semitism. Foster doesn't decree what precisely readers' responses to such texts should be - that is a personal task each reader has to decide by him/herself.

In his chapter 26 Foster describes the prevailing and even dominating effect of literary irony. If a text is written in an ironic mode, than any symbolism, associations, or traditional uses of meaning go out the window. If the text explicitly discusses a journey or quest, for instance, a literary convention that suggests growth, self-knowledge etc., but at the same time makes use of irony, then one should expect the "quest" to meaning anything but that. The "ironic mode," first formally identified by literary theorist Northrop Frye, refers to a text in which the characters possess lesser autonomy, self-determination or free will than ourselves, which means we know something they don't quite realize themselves. As readers, we also can see consequences that elude the characters in the text. In T.S. Eliot's "The Wasteland," the onset of spring ("April is the cruellest month") does nothing to revive or rejuvenate the wasteland described.

One of the characteristics of irony is its creation of the space between expectation and reality, resulting in a dual awareness on the part of the reader. Such effect or awareness is not always easy to achieve or grasp, however: at times the irony is so subtle so as to elude us of any double meaning or multiplicity to the text, character, or event in the literary work. Foster cites various examples to demonstrate this point. He also points out that irony is especially prevalent in modern and post-modernist works, which almost always challenge conventional expectations. Recognition of the use of irony can greatly reward the reading experience - it can add various dimensions to the work and challenges readers to constantly consider alternative interpretations.

In Chapter 27, as a synthesis of all the previous chapters and literary conventions described, Foster offers an analytical exercise in his final section. The text under consideration is Katherine Mansfield's short story, "The Garden Party." In addition to asking the reader to analyze the work by considering the story's message, themes, signification, literary tools and conventions employed, Fosters offers by way of example various readings of the piece, which he obtains through students and relatives, before finally providing his own interpretation of the work. The readings that Foster obtains vary from short accounts of what the story is about to more lengthy analyses of the metaphorical implications of Mansfield's work. Thus, a college freshman was able to identify the story's overall breakdown between the rich and working class, whilst a history major who had taken several of Foster's courses provided more details by identifying various themes such as an overtone of indifference, the decision to act or not, a character's struggle between her social and personal motivations and perceptions of reality.

Foster's third respondent, a graduate who took several courses in literature and creative writing provides the most comprehensive of all analyses noting not only the tension between social classes and tendencies to ignore the realities of the world, but also analyzing key metaphors such as that of birds and flight. Such imagery, pervasive throughout the text, conveys a general sense of insulation and ignorance. The respondent goes to consider how this metaphor is used to convey a character's personality and growth as the story progresses.

Foster notes how all his student-readings identify the observable phenomena of the story, which he argues is important before one can hope to analyze the more subtle aspects of the text. It is important for the reader to position him/herself in the more concrete aspects of the work so as not to produce analysis that is largely inventive and fanciful. For his own part, Foster provides what he describes as a reading at the "noumenal level," which captures the pith or essence of the story. One of the features that particularly stood out for Foster is the garden imagery as well as the use of term "ideal." The story's hyperbolic description ("perfect" day) right at the start seem to be quite suggestive, and the rather idyllic imagery used to describe the gardener and the flowers suggests a rather divine or angelic environment rather than a human one. Against this backdrop, Foster asks the question as to who is in charge - he identifies Mrs. Sheridan, the family matriarch as the head and goes on to equate her as the queen or goddess of this idyllic garden world. Her supervision of food, party decor and her children suggests to Foster parallels to a fertility goddess reigning over her kingdom.

Foster goes on to analyze other developments in the story including the increasing identification and relation between Mrs. Sheridan and the protagonist, Laura (her daughter), as well as the dark imagery associated with Laura's trip to her neighbors down the hill who belong to the working class. A host of other striking features accompany her journey, ultimately seeming reminiscent of Greek mythology -- in particular, the journey to the underground. Foster imagines that Laura and her trip represent the tale of Persephone and Demeter. The latter is the goddess of agriculture, fertility and marriage whose daughter Persephone, captured by the god of the underworld is forced to go down to visit Hell. Foster acknowledges other elements of the myth/story as well such as Laura's initiation into adulthood and acquiring of knowledge.

Foster concludes by noting that a literal understanding of the story without recognizing deeper allusions and imagery is still a great and necessary starting point - the reader has to be able to reach this stage to then identify more subtle implications of the text which would lead to conclusions similar or different from his own or his students', but which nonetheless will enrich the reading experience. Ultimately, Mansfield's short story contains several significations including a critique of the class system, initiation in adult world of death and sex, family dynamics, and a child struggling with her independent personality under the influence of her parents.

Analysis:

Foster's final few chapters emphasize the varying ways in which literature can be approached. The chapter "Don't Read With Your Eyes" highlights one of these ways: keeping in mind the characters standpoint/position and adds to other perspectives outlined in the book - socio-historic context, author's background, personal response and instinct. The point is not to overwhelm the student but rather to demonstrate how reading is a multi-layered, complex process. Literary analysis too, is similarly nonlinear. Rather than attempting to recall all approached to literature the reader should instead consider which approach is most meaningful for him/her, and keep in mind that alternative models and theories always exist. Such diversity points to the richness of even a single story or poem - as well as, ultimately, of our lives and human experience.

Although in his discussion of irony Foster describes characters as possessing less autonomy or freedom - of the audience knowing more than the characters - it is also entirely possible for an ironic piece to misdirect the reader. In his book *Literary Irony and the Literary Audience,* John B. McKee focuses on this particular mode of ironic writing. Pointing out that it is difficult to reach to a single definition of irony, he describes the type of deliberate irony that his work focuses on as cases where "misunderstandings are designed by the artist to form part of the process by which the reader comes to a final understanding of the art-work." Examples of such writing include *Tom Jones, Gulliver's Travels,* and *Tristram Shandy.* It is also helpful to know that this sort of deliberate irony for readers (what McKee calls the "reader-victimization") emerged more or less with the emergence of the novel. Earlier works such as Shakespeare were likely to employ irony as Foster describes it - where characters misunderstand whilst the audience or readers recognizes the truth.

Irony can be used for various effects - it can be employed for comic purposes, satirical effect or to heighten tragedy. Whatever the intention, irony ultimately points to the human capacity for error - or for blindness. It underscores how easily men and women, blinded by their own narrow point of view, fail to recognize that they are part of a much larger/bigger world. It can also indicate our limited nature, our tendencies to overlook or not recognize everyday phenomenon. Irony need not be severe in its message, but it helps remind us of human fallibility, and the need perhaps for greater humility and understanding in our lives.

Fosters' students' analysis of Katherine Mansfield's "The Garden Party" can help demonstrate to the reader just how many readings of a text there can be - and how all are equally valid. Readers engage with texts for various reasons, because of different literary elements/conventions. The final students' analysis for instance reveals how the bird imagery particularly stuck out for her - and deeper study of this theme led to further insights into plot, characters, and structure. Although the student didn't focus on many other elements within the text - such as parallels to Greek mythology, or the Edenic references, her analysis was still quite rich.

As Foster shares his own perspectives of the story the reader should note how this is an example of multiple readings generating additional revelations, and a work becomes richer in light of all the different understandings/readings. Often the works we enjoy the most are ones that resonate most with us - literary analysis is a way of understanding how texts can be resonant for others. Such an understanding can in turn enable students to identify with works in novel ways, ultimately fostering appreciation of the work in question, and hopefully for the literary tradition as a whole.

How to Read Literature Like a Professor Symbols, Allegory and Motifs

The Pilgrim's Progess (Allegory)

Foster cites John Bunyan's 1678 work *The Pilgrim's Progress* to give an example of an allegorical work. In Bunyan's tale, characters represent a particular thought, theme, or idea largely relating to religion and one's journey. For instance, the main protagonist, Christian, is actually meant to represent followers of Christianity seeking truth - other fictive characters and allegories include Faith, the Evangelist, Despair, etc.

"Their names indicate their qualities, and in the case of Despair, his size as well. Allegories have one mission to accomplish - convey a certain message, in this case, the quest of the devout Christian to reach heaven" (p 98, Chapter 12 - Is That a Symbol?).

Caves - A Passage to India (Symbol)

Foster identifies caves as a prime example of symbols in E.M. Foster's *A Passage to India*. Here caves can take on multiple meanings according to various characters' interactions with them. Possible meanings include: a means of accessing innermost subconscious; colonialism and hypocrisy; fear and darkness.

"The only thing we are sure of about the cave as symbol is that it keeps its secrets...What the cave symbolizes will be determined to a large extent by how the individual reader engages the text" (p 102-103, Chapter 12 - Is That a Symbol?).

River (Symbol)

Foster cites the example of river as symbol to illustrate how writers choose to emphasize various aspects of symbolic interpretations of a single symbol. River, for instance, is used to represent both danger and safety, journey and self-growth, freedom and escape in Mark Twain's *The Adventures of Huckleberry Finn*. In Hart Crane's poem "The Bridge," the river is a connector as well as divider between the northern, eastern, southern and western parts of America - in short, an important network.

"The problem of symbolic meaning is further compounded when we look at a number of writers emphasizing various, distinct elements for a given symbol. As an example, let's consider three rivers. Mark Twain gives us the Mississippi, Hart Crane the Hudson-East-Mississippi/generic-American, and T.S. Eliot the Thames" (p 103, Chapter 12 - Is That a Symbol?).

Mowing - "Out, Out - " (Symbol)

Robert Frost accords symbolic value to an action (rather than an object or image) in his poem, "Out, out - ". Here Foster considers how mowing can be a stand in for labor, solitude, and even the fragility of human life.

"...mowing carries weight beyond its immediate context, seeming to stand in for labor generally, or for the solitary business of living one's life, or for something else beyond itself" (p 105- 106, Chapter 12 - Is That a Symbol?).

Road - "The Road Not Taken" (Symbol)

Another instance of symbolic action is decision making such as indicated by the persona in Robert Frost's "The Road Not Taken."

Two roads diverged in a wood, and I—
I took the one less traveled by,
And that has made all the difference.

In this poem, the divergence of paths or the road motif comes to represent human decision making, and the persona's words comes to represent, largely, the significance of moments of decision in human lives. The words become symbolic of themes such as free will, agency, freedom and independence amongst other human concerns (p 106, Chapter 12 - Is That a Symbol?).

How to Read Literature Like a Professor Metaphors and Similes

N/A

--

N/A

--

N/A

--

N/A

--

N/A

--

How to Read Literature Like a Professor Irony

Books - "Howards End"

In E.M. Forster's novel "Howards End," books, which are conventionally sources and symbols of knowledge or enlightenment, bring about the protagonist's downfall. Leonard Bast is a working class man who strives to better himself by reading socially approved books on art and culture, attending lectures and concerts etc. His attempts to ascend the social ladder are successful, but bring about misery and wretchedness rather than happiness. In the end, when the character collapses of a heart attack, he finds he has pulled a bookcase over on himself.

"We would normally see his love of books as something that is affirming of values, improving, and educational - all of which we know as positive virtues. As Leonard collapses, however, the last thing he sees are the books from the bookcase he has pulled over on himself. We sense the disjunction between what books ought to be and the function assigned to them here by Forster" (p 241, Chapter 26: Is He Serious? And Other Ironies).

Rain - "A Farewell to Arms"

Ernest Hemingway's *A Farewell to Arms* is a ironic work, a theme suggested by the title itself. "A Farewell" was a poem written by George Peele about soldiers enthusiastically responding to call to war, and the opening two words of the poem were "To arms!" By joining these two phrases Hemingway created a title very different in meaning.

Rain, which is traditionally seen as purifying or uplifting, is used in an ironic sense in this novel. The protagonist, Frederic Henry, after experiencing the death of his lover and her baby during childbirth, walks out into the rain. Foster describes how,

"Frederic Henry walks out into rain in a season that is still winter but comes on the heels of a false spring. There's nothing cleansing or rejuvenating about the whole thing" (p 237, Chapter 26: Is He Serious? And Other Ironies).

Road - "Waiting for Godot"

In Samuel Beckett's *Waiting for Godot* the quest or journey motif is overturned on its head. The play presents two characters, Vladimir and Estragon, besides a road that they never take. Although they return to the same spot every day, the person they wait for does not ever come; nor does the road offer anything interesting for them.

Foster analyzes the irony in the story:

"Of course we catch on pretty fast and soon understand that the road exists for Didi and Gogo to take, and that their inability to do so indicates a colossal failure to engage life...Here are two men, Didi and Gogo, who wish to find possibilities for change or improvement, yet they can only understand the road they wait beside passively, in terms of what it brings to them. We in the audience can see the implication that eludes them (this is where our expectations concerning roads enter the equation), so much so that we may want to scream at them to walk up the road to a new life. But of course they never do" (p 236, Chapter 26: Is He Serious? And Other Ironies).

Arrow - "The Arrow of Heaven"

In G.K. Chesterton's "The Arrow of Heaven," traditional expectations of what an arrow is and how it should perform are undermined. The mystery story relays the killing of a man by an arrow. The victim, however, was in a high tower with higher windows, which would make a straight shot impossible except if it was from the skies or heaven. The solution turns out to be surprisingly straightforward, however: the arrow was used to stab the victim, which could be done by anyone in the same room or in close proximity. We are blinded to unusual uses of an arrow because of our preconceptions of how an arrow normally works.

"Our expectations about the arrow, like those of the characters in the story, point us in one direction, but Chesterton deflects the meaning away from those expectations. Mysteries, like irony, make great use of deflection. The arrow itself is stable; arrows are arrows. The uses to which arrows can be put and the meanings we attach to them, however, are not so stable" (p 239, Chapter 26: Is He Serious? And Other Ironies).

How to Read Literature Like a Professor Imagery

N/A

--

N/A

--

N/A

--

N/A

--

How to Read Literature Like a Professor Envoi

As a brief conclusion, Foster clarifies that his intent in writing an instructional guide for students of literature is not to identify all the codes/conventions by which literature is written and understood. The literary features he analyzes in this book are only a few of a variety of tropes, motifs, and literary tools employed by writers and seen in texts. The book instead hopes to provide a general template and guide that can enable the reader to begin to look for and use literary codes on their own. He also states that one does not need to know or read all conventions - enough familiarity with the basics can eventually enable the identification of patterns and symbols to become second nature during reading. Foster also offers suggestions for further reading in his Appendix, but encourages the reader to find works that resonate particularly with them and which allow them to enjoy literature above anything else.

Foster's reading list is divided into Primary Works of Literature, Fairytales, Movies, Secondary Sources of Literature, and Master Class.

How to Read Literature Like a Professor Literary Elements

Genre

Non-Fiction

Setting and Context

Guide on English Literature

Narrator and Point of View

First-Person perspective of author, Thomas C. Foster

Tone and Mood

Analytical and engaging; formal when discussing literary features and elements, and informal when explaining them.

Protagonist and Antagonist

N/A

Major Conflict

N/A

Climax

N/A

Foreshadowing

N/A

Understatement

N/A

Allusions

N/A

Imagery

N/A

Paradox

N/A

Parallelism

N/A

Metonymy and Synecdoche

English Literature - Novels, Poems, Sonnets, Plays from classical to contemporary times written in or translated to English

Personification

N/A

How to Read Literature Like a Professor Links

Author's Official Website

http://thomascfoster.com/

Official website of Thomas C. Foster, including brief autobiography, present work, publications and contact

Review of "How To Read"

http://classiclit.about.com/cs/productreviews/fr/aafpr_howtoread.htm

Concise review on the redeeming features of *How to Read.*

Wikipedia on "How to Read"

https://en.wikipedia.org/wiki/How_to_Read_Literature_Like_a_Professor

Brief Wikipedia entry on the book and its author.

HarperCollins Speakers Bureau

http://www.harpercollinsspeakersbureau.com/speaker/thomas-c-foster/

HarperCollins, which has published many of Foster's works has an entry on the author which includes his biography, credentials, and areas of expertise.

UMichigan-Flint official profile

https://www.umflint.edu/english/facstaff_profiles/foster

Dr. Thomas Foster's profile at the university (University of Michigan-Flint) at which he taught and received title of Professor Emeritus of English.

How to Read Literature Like a Professor Essay Questions

1. **Discuss the possible implications of Christian and Biblical imagery to a literary work, and the importance of such imagery to literary analysis.**

    Possible implications could include continuation of historic traditions, relationship to our past, time and its progression. It would also certainly suggest Divinity and sanctity, spirituality, our beholdenness to Fate. The Bible as a work of authority is also used in literature to lend authority to the text and the story. From a literary point of view it is important because of the prevailing influence of Christianity and monotheism in Western culture (there could other reasons as well).

2. **Describe the complexities of the relationship between setting and character.**

    A good answer would not only point to ways in which complexity is created because of the non-linear relationship between character and setting - humans affect places as much as places affect us - but also describe ways in which this occurs. Thus, the answer could consider how geography can play a role in developing character's motives or else personality, such as through inspiring a desire to escape. At the same time, human actions and their significance can be understood through a study of nature and surroundings such as the polluted lanscape's indication of modernization and industrialization.

3. **Name at least two canonical works that are among the most often cited/reproduced (according to Foster), and give examples of how different forms that references to these works can take.**

    One of the collections widely known is that of Shakespearean plays and sonnets, whilst another could be Greek mythology (or the Bible). Writers have often used Shakespearean characters as archetypes almost as a way of highlighting their own character's personality traits - reference to Hamlet for instance might convey a particular figure's inability to act or else famililial issues. Dialogue from Shakespearean plays and sonnets also abound in literature as well as popular culture - phrases such as "All the world's a stage" that have achieved immense popularity because of their universal quality and commentary on human existence. Similarly, Greek mythological stories have been modified throughout the centuries, with themes as popular as mother-son relationships, narcissm, and so forth. Greek names continue to be used often as a means of indicating personality traits/archetypes (Homer, Oedipia, etc.)

4. **Identify at least three theories regarding of literary analysis.**

These could include reader-response theory, which considers the reader's response to the text and his/her ascription of meaning to the work; deconstruction, an approach that considers the work to be a product of various social, historic, political and macro factors rather than an independent production of the writer; and finally, intertextuality, which sees literary works as engaging in dialogue with one another (references and parallels with other stories in a particular work of fiction).

5. **Which skills does Foster think need to be developed in order for one to become a better reader and student of literature?**

A good answer will consider the complexity of the question as well as answer - what precisely makes a "good" reader/student? Literature is a complex field as is reading itself; although Foster does identify specific practices early on such as pattern recognition, memory, and ability to read symbolically, the relationship between reader and text is never straightforward. Other important considerations include contextualizing, considering the author's position and perspective, re-reading works as well. There is no definitive answer here, responses also depend largely on your own views on what literature and reading should be like. Whilst it is okay to take a specific stance, you must defend it well.

How to Read Literature Like a Professor Quizzes

1. **In Raymond Carver's "Cathedral" Foster describes the characters' actions of consuming a joint as a form of communion because:**
   A. At least one of the character is devout
   B. They partake in a ritual that creates social and community bonds
   C. It is a stand-in for a meal
   D. Symbolically, a joint or drug has long carried spiritual or trancedental meaning

2. **Of the following characteristics, what is not typically associated with vampires/Dracula?**
   A. Garlic
   B. Allure and sexuality
   C. Selfishness
   D. Spirituality and condemnation

3. **In James Joyce's "The Dead," the imagery associated with the dinner table most strongly suggests which of the following themes?**
   A. Communion and sharing
   B. Life and Death
   C. Battle and arms
   D. Decadence and Luxury

4. **"Two gazed into a pool, he gazed and she, Not hand in hand but heart in heart I think, Pale and reluctant on the water's brink" What kind of meter/rhythm does Christina Rosetti's sonnet incorporate?**
   A. Octave, unstressed, stressed, stressed, unstressed syllable
   B. Octave, stressed and unstressed syllable
   C. Decasyllable, stressed and unstressed
   D. Decasyllable, stressed, unstressed, unstressed, stressed

5. **The title "The Sound and the Fury" pays homage to which of the following literary writers?**
   A. Hamlet
   B. Angela Carter
   C. William Shakespeare
   D. William Faulkner

6. **References to the Bible or Shakespeare in a literary work can achieve all of the following except,**
> A. Indicate contemporary relevance of ancient values and themes
> B. Undermine expectations
> C. Confer an authority to the story and writing
> D. Indicate an author's religious and political leaning

7. **Of the following, which is NOT a quality that Foster thinks makes for a good story:**
> A. 'Political' writing
> B. Familiarity and strangeness
> C. A mimicry/slavish emulation of a character from another work such as Brothers Grimm Fairytales
> D. Allusions to older works

8. **In his discussion on the lasting influence of myth, Foster is referring specifically to which of the following?**
> A. Graeco-Roman traditional sources
> B. Stories of communities
> C. Greek philosophers (such as Plato and Socrates') writings
> D. Arabian Nights

9. **Rain in a work of literature can most strongly suggest which of the following**
> A. Intertextuality
> B. Satire
> C. Growth and cleansing
> D. Tears

10. **"The Wasteland's" (T.S Eliot) opening lines are ironic because**
> A. April is actually symbolically the happiest month
> B. April showers can be grim and overwhelming
> C. Expectations people have from Spring are never quite met
> D. April is the month of spring and hope

11. **The "Intentionalist" writers differ from their contemporaries in that they:**
> A. Do not pay close attention to the external sources they draw upon in their stories/writing
> B. Write in the mythic rather than narrative methos
> C. Intend, to the extent possible, all effects in their writing
> D. They hail from the modernist period

12. **Violence in literature can possibly indicate all of the following except:**
> A. Fragility of our lives
> B. Cruelty of the universe and nature
> C. Fertility and agriculture
> D. A society's failure or oppressiveness

13. **In mystery novels, according to Foster, death operates differently in that:**
        A. It leads to emotional satisfaction and weightiness
        B. It leads to questions and riddles and/or mystery
        C. It is the reason for the story to exist in the first place
        D. It is not very significant in and of itself

14. **An example of a literary symbol is:**
        A. A newspaper's use of pictorial suns/clouds in its weather report
        B. The "tree" carved on Sethe's back through whipping in Toni Morrison's "Beloved."
        C. Character of Christian in John Bunyan's "The Pilgrim's Progress"
        D. A story containing fantasy or magic such as Harry Potter

15. **Foster recommends that the reader should read symbollically in the following ways EXCEPT**
        A. Act on initial suspicions and inclinations
        B. Consider various meanings of the object/image and their relevance to the context at hand
        C. Search for possible meanings of a particular image/object and use the 5 most common/popular results in interpreting the symbol
        D. Read various works so as to familiarize oneself with ways in which literary symbolism is used

16. **The difference between political and 'political' writing can be illustrated by which of the following analogies:**
        A. NYTimes article on US-Iran talks and an Op-Ed on the social implications of US-Iran relations
        B. Ezra Pound's Anti-Semitist poetry and T.S Eliot's post world war poems
        C. Socialist Realist novels and a NYTimes article on US-Iran talks
        D. Socialist Realist novels and Virginia Woolf's "Mrs. Dalloway"

17. **In which of the following contexts and traditions is the Christ Figure most likely to feature?**
        A. Greek or Roman mythology
        B. Anne Bradstreet and other Puritan New World poets
        C. Tales from the Arabian Nights
        D. "Moth Smoke" and other novels by Pakistani author Mohsin Hamid

18. **Flight in literature can be a symbolic extention of:**
    A. The difference between air-borne creatures and humans
    B. All humans' subconscious desires from the very beginning of time
    C. Evolution from land-ridden creatures to birds
    D. Escape and freedom

19. **Foster devotes a chapter to Baptism in order to explain**
    A. How prevalent the Christian tradition is in literature
    B. How writers use it to convey man's complex relationship with the divine
    C. How baptism is still considered a sacred and necessary ritual even by liberal Christians
    D. How drowning/submersion in water is symbolic of rebirth for characters

20. **Setting can convey all of the following in a work of literature except,**
    A. The author's most preferred location/region
    B. Social and political commentary
    C. Man's influence on nature and vice versa
    D. A character's motives/decisions/development

21. **"That time of year thou mayst in me behold/ When yellow leaves or none or few do hang" What can be gleamed from these verses of Shakespearean sonnet regarding the literary implications of season?**
    A. Seasonal imagery makes heavy use of the image of trees to indicate a person
    B. "Yellow Leaves" were always used by traditional writers to indicate the coming of Autumn
    C. That the ways in which a character is described can be used to understand what time of the year/ season it is
    D. Writers can associate seasons with human life such as autumn ("yellow leaves") which often indicaes the onset of age and decline

22. **According to Foster pure originality is:**
    A. Impossible largely because in the end, there is really only one story.
    B. Possible but does not make for respectable literature
    C. Impossible because writers know they have to include elements of familiarity for their works to become enjoyed
    D. Possible if the writer grows up without reading any of the great literary works

23. **Harry Potter's scar can indicate all of the following except:**
   A. That the work is part of a fantastical genre
   B. Harry is distinct from other wizards and witches
   C. Some wounds - such as dark magic and death of his parents - never heal
   D. A physical manifestation of the connection between him and Voldemort

24. **Blindness is a literary novel can have the following symbolic implications except:**
   A. Irony
   B. That there is more than what meets the eye
   C. An indication of the number of visually-impaired in the society which the author draws inspiration from for the setting of his novel
   D. That one can be blind in understanding to situations/facts in front of them

25. **According to Foster literature should be:**
   A. Written by authors well versed and trained in caonical works
   B. Approached only from a deconstructionist methodology so as to lead to a rich analysis and reading experience
   C. Enjoyable for the reader
   D. Only analyzed when its conventions learnt

Quiz 1 Answer Key

1. **(B)** They partake in a ritual that creates social and community bonds
2. **(D)** Spirituality and condemnation
3. **(C)** Battle and arms
4. **(C)** Decasyllable, stressed and unstressed
5. **(C)** William Shakespeare
6. **(D)** Indicate an author's religious and political leaning
7. **(C)** A mimicry/slavish emulation of a character from another work such as Brothers Grimm Fairytales
8. **(A)** Graeco-Roman traditional sources
9. **(C)** Growth and cleansing
10. **(D)** April is the month of spring and hope
11. **(C)** Intend, to the extent possible, all effects in their writing
12. **(C)** Fertility and agriculture
13. **(D)** It is not very significant in and of itself
14. **(B)** The "tree" carved on Sethe's back through whipping in Toni Morrison's "Beloved."
15. **(C)** Search for possible meanings of a particular image/object and use the 5 most common/popular results in interpreting the symbol
16. **(D)** Socialist Realist novels and Virginia Woolf's "Mrs. Dalloway"
17. **(B)** Anne Bradstreet and other Puritan New World poets
18. **(D)** Escape and freedom
19. **(D)** How drowning/submersion in water is symbolic of rebirth for characters
20. **(A)** The author's most preferred location/region
21. **(D)** Writers can associate seasons with human life such as autumn ("yellow leaves") which often indicaes the onset of age and decline
22. **(A)** Impossible largely because in the end, there is really only one story.
23. **(A)** That the work is part of a fantastical genre
24. **(C)** An indication of the number of visually-impaired in the society which the author draws inspiration from for the setting of his novel
25. **(C)** Enjoyable for the reader

How to Read Literature Like a Professor Quizzes

1. **In Judith Guest's "Ordinary People," the metaphor of drowning is used in which of the following ways?**
    A. As a means of underscoring the older brother's inability to survive the trials of life
    B. A point of rebirth and re-creation of the self for the younger brother
    C. The younger brother's physical, and eventually, moral superiority
    D. Human life's dependence on Nature and Fate

2. **A character traveling South is likely to:**
    A. Bring his Northern prejudices
    B. Be involved in dramatic adventure
    C. Suffer from tropical disease
    D. Be a symbol of colonialism

3. **According to Foster, knowledge of which of the following elements is important for an appreciation of Seamus Heaney's "Bogland" and depiction of Northern Island?**
    A. Politics during Heaney"s time
    B. Theodore Roethke "In Praise of Prairie"
    C. The geographical landscape of bogs and turf
    D. Ancient history of Northern Island

4. **Which of the following seasons can be indicative of happiness and misery, respectively?**
    A. Autumn and Summer
    B. Spring and Summer
    C. Spring and Winter
    D. Autumn and Spring

5. **In Henry James' "Daisy Miller" is what ways does the protagonist, Daisy's name carry significance?**
    A. The simple/straightforward name suggests the difference in American culture from that of European - the simplicity of social bonds in contrast with the rigidity of European customs
    B. It captures the personality of the character - her youth and freshness - through allusions to Spring
    C. It indicates her beauty and goddess-like features through reference to mythological flowers
    D. It indicates the simple background she comes from as the daughter of a hardworking miller

6. **Interpreting Hamlet through the lens of modern psychological diagnosis of cancer would be an example of:**
   A. Blind spot
   B. Deconstructivist approach
   C. Modernist analysis
   D. Enriching the reading experience by offering varying perspectives

7. **The various episodes involving concubines in "The Iliad" should, according to Foster, be interpreted as:**
   A. Proof of the reigning culture of sexuality
   B. An age-old practice no longer relevant
   C. A deeply ingrained local tradition that has significant implications/meaning
   D. Aspects of Greek culture that should be condemned even if they feature in notable literature

8. **In an ironic work, an opening sentence which states "Once upon a time" could suggest:**
   A. That the story will have anything but a fairytale ending
   B. That the work is a children's story
   C. That the work hopes to reach out to a wider audience by drawing on familiar literary elements
   D. That the work is heavily influenced by Brothers Grimm

9. **The following are said to be twentieth-century masters of the ironic stance:**
   A. Samuell Beckett, T. Coraghessan Boyle, Angela Carter
   B. Samuell Beckett, Angela Carter, Friedrich Schlegel,
   C. Lord Byron, James Joyce, Vladimir Nabokov
   D. Vladimir Nabokov, William Wordsworth, Franz Kafka

10. **In Katherine Mansfield's "The Garden Party" the main narrative perspective is that of:**
    A. Second person perspective
    B. Omniscient narrator
    C. First person perspective
    D. Third person perspective and Laura, the daughter

11. **Which of the following is a principle governing the use of disease in literature according to Foster?**
    A. How a character acquires a disease is an important part of the narrative
    B. Some diseases are given preference over others
    C. A disease should primarily have 3 implications: personal, social, and moral
    D. Diseases should be romanticized to the point of beauty

12. **What was the prime disease for the Romantics and Victorians according to Foster's analysis?**
        A. Cholera
        B. Tuberculosis
        C. Consumption
        D. AIDS

13. **Dickens uses fever in his works in all of the following ways except:**
        A. To cause another character's heartbreak
        B. To point to a disease that was widespread in London at the time
        C. To dispose of the many characters that existed in his work
        D. For narrative suspense

14. **Foster would agree with which of the following statements about author James Baldwin's intent with his short story "Sonny's Blues?"**
        A. Sonny's addiction is a commentary on the struggles faced by lower-middle class America at the time
        B. The story suggests pitfalls in a recovering addict's journey
        C. The story is ultimately a resolution of Sonny's struggles
        D. Sonny's addiction is not as central a theme as redemption

15. **In an ironic mode characters:**
        A. Are more than what they are overtly described as
        B. Exercise limited expression of free will and/or independence
        C. Are self-conscious of themselves and the events which unfold
        D. Are often satirical

16. **Ernest Hemingway's poem "A Farewell to Arms" is ironic because**
        A. Because they condemn the practice of warfare
        B. They relate a 16th century work to the modernist period
        C. They are inspired by George Peele's poem
        D. They imply the opposite of the original meaning of the source they were drawn from

17. **The following is an example of a signifier and signified (respectively)**
        A. A book representing wisdom
        B. A thermometer showing the temperature/weather
        C. A dog representing animals
        D. Snow representing winter

18. **The following is an ironic example of signifier and signified:**
        A. A boat which leads its passengers into an adventerous journey and voyage
        B. A baby whose birth marks a new chapter in the household/ family's state of affairs
        C. Snow which indicates the cold bitterness prevailing
        D. A book which, when read, misguides the reader from truth

19. The statement "her hair has gone quite gold from grief" in Oscar
    Wilde's "The Importance of Being Earnest" is most appropriately
    categorized as:
    > A. Allegory
    > B. Comic irony
    > C. Parody
    > D. Metaphor

20. In "Mrs. Dalloway" the description of the two doctors which come to
    treat the war veteran Septimus Warren Smith are described as the
    "enemies." This is ironic because:
    > A. The doctors are well-trained professionals in their field
    > B. The enemy turns out to be individuals from the war veteran's
    > own community
    > C. Septimus is mentally disturbed and doesn't realize what he
    > says
    > D. The doctors are actually veterans themselves

21. The following can be gleamed from an initial reading of Katherine
    Mansfield's "The Garden Party" except:
    > A. Subtle undertones of Greek Underworld and a young girl's
    > acquisition of knowledge of sexuality
    > B. Class divisions and insulated life of the upper class
    > C. Bird imagery and flight
    > D. Idealized/Edenic references

22. A twentieth-century writer was more likely to select tuberculosis over
    cholera as a disease in his work because:
    > A. Cholera had a moral taboo associated with it
    > B. Cholera was not as aggressive as tuberculosis
    > C. There are painful and unappealing stigmas associated with
    > Cholera
    > D. Tuberculosis was more widespread

23. The following are instances of irony in Oedipus Rex except:
    > A. Tiresias the seer is able to grasp and see the truth for what it is
    > B. Oedipus has a wounded foot and is marked from the rest
    > C. Oedipus is unable to realize the truth and comprehend reality
    > when he is a ruler and possesses his sight
    > D. Towards the end of Oedipus' life, despite his blindness, he
    > acquires a keen level of vision

24. Richard III scolosis in Shakespeare's "Richard III" represents all the
    following except:
    > A. His deplorable character
    > B. His differentiation from the rest
    > C. Divine displeasure/condemnation
    > D. A horrific illness in Elizebethan times

25. **The reason intertextuality works so well is because:**

A. The great body of literature including myths, archetypes and spiritual narratives are part of our collective consciousnness

B. The subconscious is always active during reading

C. Each century modifies previous years' works

D. Writers are well read themselves

Quiz 2 Answer Key

1. **(B)** A point of rebirth and re-creation of the self for the younger brother
2. **(B)** Be involved in dramatic adventure
3. **(C)** The geographical landscape of bogs and turf
4. **(C)** Spring and Winter
5. **(B)** It captures the personality of the character - her youth and freshness - through allusions to Spring
6. **(A)** Blind spot
7. **(C)** A deeply ingrained local tradition that has significant implications/ meaning
8. **(A)** That the story will have anything but a fairytale ending
9. **(A)** Samuell Beckett, T. Coraghessan Boyle, Angela Carter
10. **(D)** Third person perspective and Laura, the daughter
11. **(B)** Some diseases are given preference over others
12. **(C)** Consumption
13. **(B)** To point to a disease that was widespread in London at the time
14. **(D)** Sonny's addiction is not as central a theme as redemption
15. **(B)** Exercise limited expression of free will and/or independence
16. **(D)** They imply the opposite of the original meaning of the source they were drawn from
17. **(A)** A book representing wisdom
18. **(D)** A book which, when read, misguides the reader from truth
19. **(B)** Comic irony
20. **(B)** The enemy turns out to be individuals from the war veteran's own community
21. **(A)** Subtle undertones of Greek Underworld and a young girl's acquisition of knowledge of sexuality
22. **(C)** There are painful and unappealing stigmas associated with Cholera
23. **(B)** Oedipus has a wounded foot and is marked from the rest
24. **(D)** A horrific illness in Elizebethan times
25. **(A)** The great body of literature including myths, archetypes and spiritual narratives are part of our collective consciousnness

How to Read Literature Like a Professor Quizzes

1. **"Now is the winter of our discontent,/Made glorious summer by this son of York" The following literary elements can be found in this Shakespearean quote except:**
   A. Pun
   B. Foreshadowing
   C. Seasonal imagery
   D. Sarcasm

2. **W.H Auden's "In Praise of Limestone" primarily does which of the following?**
   A. Present geography that is habitable
   B. Carry forward the views of his predecessors
   C. Lament the detrimental effects of human action on nature
   D. Sing praise of nature's natural resources

3. **In Toni Morrison's "Beloved" the river achives which of the following:**
   A. Convey a sense of purification and cleansing
   B. Convey symbolic baptism through drowning and resurfacing that works on personal, cultural and racial levels
   C. Transport the daughter Beloved from the underworld to Earth
   D. Mark the protagonist's home

4. **A writer hoping to convey sexuality/sex might do which of the following?**
   A. Use some of many cliches that have risen from previous works' descriptions of sex
   B. Suggest something through explicit dialogue
   C. Present a scene of violence between the characters
   D. Describe the act in subtle, brief, non-cliche ways

5. **In Gabriel Garcia Marquez's "A Very Old Man with Enormous Wings" how does the trope of flight function?**
   A. Suggests rebirth and salvation
   B. Conveys beauty and sublimity
   C. Signals possibilities of freedom
   D. As an ironic trope

6. **Allusions to Christ figure in a literary work may likely do all of the following except:**
    A. Reinforce a character's sacrifice
    B. Assert superiority of Christian tradition over other monotheistic faiths
    C. Make a character seem great or divine
    D. Make a character look smaller

7. **The following are literary effects of a predominantly Christian culture except**
    A. Baptism imagery
    B. The Christ archetype
    C. References to Greek mythological tradition
    D. The widespread presence of Biblical discourse (quotes, stories, dialogues)

8. **What are the political implications of Edger Allen Poe's "The Fall of the House of Usher" according to Foster?**
    A. The long, esteemed tradition of European monarchy
    B. American aristocracy's ills
    C. The complex relationship between Europe and America
    D. A decaying, corrupt social organization in Europe

9. **Foster suggests that Charles Dickens' "A Christmas Carol" is so popular in part because:**
    A. The character of Scrooge is a fascinating novelty
    B. The story is meant to change us and society
    C. The character of Scrooge is relatable and representative
    D. It has significant moral lessons

10. **Engaging our creative intelligence involves:**
    A. Thinking deeply about the socio-historic context in which the work was written
    B. Researching the writer's background and philosophy as much as possible to understand his perspective and then see the work through his eyes
    C. Imagining the possibilities that are contained in the story
    D. Paying attention to instinctive responses to the text

11. **Robert Frost's "The Road Not Taken" is symbolic of:**
    A. Difficult travels
    B. Places that have not been visited before
    C. Determination and fortitude in one's life
    D. Unknown bodies of knowledge

12. **George Orwell's "Animal Farm" functions in which of the following ways according to Foster and why?**

> A. As an allegory - it is evident what things are meant to represent
> B. As a political piece that considers pros and cons of certain systems of governance
> C. As an allegory - because the work directly discusses revolution and politics
> D. Symbolically because the features have layers of possible interpretations

13. **In reading where does a sense of weightiness come from according to Foster?**

> A. When there is a scene of violence
> B. When acts or features live on the narrative surface
> C. When there are deeper implications to what is being described in the text
> D. When there is no use of irony

14. **How can a writer hoping to draw parallels to ancient Greek culture do so in his/her writing?**

> A. Set the story in 3/4th century BC
> B. Use Graeco-Roman names such as Helen, Achille
> C. Include Elizabethan dialogue/text
> D. Use flood imagery

15. **An effect of drawing parallels between working class laborers and Greek mythological characters such as Zeus in a contemporary work of fiction would be to:**

> A. To suggest that working class laborers are gods in their own right in modern times
> B. To suggest that Greek mythology is deeply steeped in our conscienceness
> C. To suggest that the characters enjoyed Greek mythology
> D. Emphasize the traditional belief that we're all descended from gods and the potential for greatness exists in us all

16. **Pattern recognition in professorial reading is:**

> A. Reading at the response level
> B. Taking a broad view of the text to ascertain larger trends in addition to reading the details
> C. Going back and re-reading to look for general patterns after having completed the first reading
> D. Ascertaining how the details fit into larger patterns of the text

17. **A quest tale can consist of all the following except:**
    A. A romantic interest
    B. A destination
    C. A real reason to embark on the journey
    D. A quester

18. **Foster equates the character of Frederick Winterbourne in Henry James' "Daisy Miller" to which of the following personalities and why?**
    A. The Knight archetype in an ironic sense because of his failure to 'save' Daisy
    B. Vampiric persona because of his cold rigidness and stifling disapproval
    C. Christ figure in an ironic sense because of his age
    D. Frakenstein because of his mechanical, hollow persona

19. **The following could be examples of literary vampires except:**
    A. A shopkeeper who tampers with the scales
    B. A teacher who gives after-school detention to a student who talked in class
    C. A father who demands perfection from his children, and ignores them when they don't perform
    D. A board of governors that pressurizes the CEO to invest in a company of their interests

20. **How might a postmodern sonnet differ from a Petrarchan sonnet?**
    A. They are ironical, and thus challenge traditional organization
    B. They do not employ a rhyme scheme at all
    C. They are divided into quatrains rather than an octave and sester
    D. The meaning of the first eight lines may continue on in the next few verses

21. **How does Angela Carter modify Shakespeare's Ophelia in her own work "Wise Children" through the character Tiffany?**
    A. She suffers greatly
    B. She takes on a dual Shakespearean role, resembling the character Hero as well
    C. She drowns in a poignant fashion
    D. She loses her mind to her father's death

22. **A writer who includes allusions to Shakespeare in his writing might hope to achieve which of the following:**
        A. Make his writing highbrow and accessible to a select audience
        B. Point to a continuity in tradition from the time of Christ (who heavily influenced Shakespeare)
        C. Lend his work an authority
        D. Draw parallels between Elizabethan times and his own to demonstrate the continuity of language

23. **A literary work that quotes dialogue from the TV series "Friends" is likely to be:**
        A. Slapstick in nature
        B. Resonant only in contemporary times
        C. Ironical
        D. Relatable as a comedy to New Yorkers 100 years from now

24. **Those authors borrowing from previous traditions have to:**
        A. Ensure that those works are widely known
        B. Acknowledge the sources explicitly in their texts
        C. Be ironical in tone
        D. Only draw on certain elements or features to convey the desired effect

25. **Shakespeare wrote his sonnets in the following forms:**
        A. 4/4/6
        B. 6/8
        C. 4/4/4/2
        D. 8/6

Quiz 3 Answer Key

1. **(B)** Foreshadowing
2. **(A)** Present geography that is habitable
3. **(B)** Convey symbolic baptism through drowning and resurfacing that works on personal, cultural and racial levels
4. **(C)** Present a scene of violence between the characters
5. **(D)** As an ironic trope
6. **(B)** Assert superiority of Christian tradition over other monotheistic faiths
7. **(C)** References to Greek mythological tradition
8. **(D)** A decaying, corrupt social organization in Europe
9. **(C)** The character of Scrooge is relatable and representative
10. **(D)** Paying attention to instinctive responses to the text
11. **(C)** Determination and fortitude in one's life
12. **(A)** As an allegory - it is evident what things are meant to represent
13. **(C)** When there are deeper implications to what is being described in the text
14. **(B)** Use Graeco-Roman names such as Helen, Achille
15. **(D)** Emphasize the traditional belief that we're all descended from gods and the potential for greatness exists in us all
16. **(B)** Taking a broad view of the text to ascertain larger trends in addition to reading the details
17. **(A)** A romantic interest
18. **(B)** Vampiric persona because of his cold rigidness and stifling disapproval
19. **(B)** A teacher who gives after-school detention to a student who talked in class
20. **(D)** The meaning of the first eight lines may continue on in the next few verses
21. **(B)** She takes on a dual Shakespearean role, resembling the character Hero as well
22. **(C)** Lend his work an authority
23. **(B)** Resonant only in contemporary times
24. **(D)** Only draw on certain elements or features to convey the desired effect
25. **(C)** 4/4/4/2

How to Read Literature Like a Professor Quizzes

1. **The following can be interpreted as acts of communion except:**
   A. A college senior offering a smoke to a freshman
   B. Two office workers who eat in their own cubicles
   C. A family who eats together whilst watching TV
   D. A boss that eats with his employees in the cafetaria

2. **The ghost in Hamlet appears to do the following except:**
   A. Urge Hamlet to act on somethng
   B. Convey an ominous foreboding
   C. Foretell disquiet in the kingdom
   D. Scare the audience/reader

3. **According to Foster the Victorian writers were skilled in which of the follwing and why?**
   A. Irony because of the period's discontent with the past
   B. Horror stories because of a prevailing fascination with the genre
   C. Sublimination because of heavy censorship
   D. Psychological writing because of writers suh as Henry James who pioneered works in this field

4. **In Tim O Brien's "Going After Cacciato" when a character falls through a hole in the road it suggests:**
   A. Intertextuality - Lewis Carrol's "Alice in Wonderland"
   B. Intertextuality - Shakespeare's "Hamlet"
   C. Irony because the hole leads to the type of world seen in Lewis Carrol's "Alice in Wonderland"
   D. Irony because the character is just as notorious as the Greek God of Hades, the underworld

5. **In order for harmonies to be produced through text, the text should:**
   A. Contain spiritual references either through Bible or other religious texts
   B. Convey a sense of continuity with the Graeco-Roman tradition
   C. Convey a sense of resonance through references to high literature such as Shakespeare, Milton and the Bible
   D. Convey a sense of depth and resonance through references to earlier texts

6. **Myth, as used by Foster is the following except:**
    A. Include Shakespearean, biblical and folk/fairy tale
    B. Sources of material for the modern writer
    C. Dubious in its authenticity
    D. The tradition of relaying human experience in ways other disciplines cannot

7. **Water has the following significance except:**
    A. It is related to the oxygen - our source of breath
    B. Prompts ancestral memories
    C. Is extensively referenced in th Judeo-Christian-Islamic world
    D. Speaks to us at a very basic level of being

8. **How is allegory different from symbollism**
    A. Allegory conveys less irony than symbolism
    B. Allegory is never comical whilst symbols may or may not be so
    C. Allegory was first introduced in early religious/spiritual literature whereas symbols have always been used
    D. Allegory denotes one specific meaning or message only whereas symbols can have a variety of interpretations

9. **Which of the following are skills Foster thinks differentiate the professional from the personal reader**
    A. Symbolic reading and irony
    B. Pattern recognition, symbolic reading, memory
    C. Memory, Writing, Pattern Recognition
    D. Reading, Pattern and Biblical knowledge

10. **An example of a Faustian bargain is:**
    A. When a parent promises the child chocolates if he/she remains silent at the doctor's office
    B. When a woman is offered the chance to relinquish her admission in a prestigious co-ed university in exchange for a full scholarship to another, all girls college
    C. When a thief makes a bargain with a fellow criminal to split the spoils of a future raid 50/50
    D. When a priest is offered a placement at the Vatican if he can introduce religious education in his community's schools

11. A character in a story is forced to leave her family's house in order to find someone who can improve her parents' deteriorating health. She has to travel far beyond her prairie homeland and cross the ocean - however when the time comes to embark the ship she is too daunted by the vast body of water lying before her to do so. She returns home, bringing with her a fisherman lad she happened to found who treats the sores and diseases that the fisherman community acquire during their work. What type of story would the above be, and what is its primary intent?

> A. quest tale about a young girl who seeks assistance for her family
>
> B.) A romantic tale - how the girl's love for her parents is rewarded by a romantic interest of her own
>
> C. A story about filial respect and duty - how a sense of concern for one's family can be self-revealing itself
>
> D. A quest tale about a young girl who recognizes her own limitations and fears

12. The eating scene in Henry Fielding's "Tom Jones" is described by the author as a form of communion because:

> A. It has heavy sexual implications/imagery
>
> B. It has spiritual/religious undertones
>
> C. It involves the sharing of a meal
>
> D. It describes two characters jointly sharing in an experience

13. Of the following, which can NOT be considered a unifier?

> A. Snow
>
> B. Capitalism
>
> C. Death
>
> D. Rain

14. A character can be said to have symbolic vampiric resemblance if:

> A. He is possessive of his girlfriend
>
> B. Has fair skin tone
>
> C. He demonstrates selfish, exploitative tendencies
>
> D. He sleeps late in the morning and is awake during the late hours of night during the weekends

15. The following are features of the structural component of a sonnet that can be said to be significant except for

> A. The regular rhythm of the verses are reminiscent of the cycle of life described in the poem
>
> B. Seasonal imagery in the poem that indicate the progression of human life
>
> C. The look of the sonnet resembles the compact life it describes in its verses
>
> D. The change of beat/rhythm after the octave to a slower pattern in the sestet

16. **Which of the following is a fairytale that Foster imagines to have universal appeal, and why?**
    A. Cinderella because of themes of servitude and exploitation
    B. Little Red Riding Hood because of sexual references
    C. Hansel & Gretel because of the trope of lost children
    D. The Gingerbread House because of transgression of property

17. **Fairytales differ from other literary traditions (Bible, Shakespeare) which writers borrow from in that they:**
    A. Are accessible to a wider audience
    B. They are easier to manipulate because of the reader's suspension of disbelief
    C. They are simpler to understand
    D. They were community myths of the Slavic tradition

18. **Foster describes the plot of "The Iliad" as:**
    A. A character, Achilles' anger and response
    B. A battle story between Greek leaders of old
    C. Related to the events of the Trojan War
    D. A tale of salvation for Troy

19. **How, according to Foster, does rain function in Thomas Hardy's "The Three Strangers?"**
    A. As an ominous portend, as a signal of rebirth, as a Biblical reference
    B. As a plot device, as a foreshadowing of ill/evil, as a signal of a change to come
    C. As a unifier, as a signal of rebirth, as a Biblical reference
    D. As a unifier, as a plot device, and as a means of conveying misery

20. **The following are paradoxes except:**
    A. The consuming fire comes from a branch of green tree
    B. Rain is fresh and pure coming down but mixes with mud to be become soiled on earth
    C. Snow falls from the sky in single flakes and ultimately covers everyone
    D. Rainbow appears after a refreshing rain

21. **The following (in capitilized letters) can be symbols except:**
    A. A character's often divulges her friends' secrets is diagnosed with Throat Cancer
    B. A character's Lost Book is found in her dog's kennel, and reveals further lost household items
    C. A character's Lost Books indicates her loss of access to knowledge
    D. A character who migrates to the city from her rural village finds herself addicted to new technologies such as the Smartphone that slowly chip away at her relations with family

22. **Violence in literature can differ from violence in real life in the following ways except:**
    A. Violence in literature is never just about one person hitting another
    B. Violence in literature is an act of aggression while not so in real life
    C. Violence in literature is a social and cultural commentary
    D. Violence in literature has Biblical implications

23. **Robert Frost's poem "Out, Out - " is inspired by which of the following works, and what is the principle underlying theme?**
    A. Macbeth,'s "Out out brief candle - " which points to the fragility of human existence
    B. Macbeth's "Out out brief candle - " which points to the assertion of human will over nature
    C. The Wasteland's "Lilacs out of the dead land, mixing" - which points to the paradox of life, good and evil
    D. Macbeth's "Out damned spot! Out I say - " which points to the never-vanishing stain of guilt and crime

24. **How is William Faulkner's use of violence distinct, according to Foster?**
    A. It draws on Biblical parallels
    B. It is seldom used in stories, but has lasting implications when it is used
    C. It is conditioned by the historical state of affairs/events
    D. It draws on mythic parallels

25. **Caves in E.M Foster's "A Passage to India" are said to have all of the following implications except:**
    A. They indicate the most basic and primitive elements of our nature
    B. They symbolize the underworld and Greek mythology
    C. They are a means of inflicting physical discomfort
    D. They are a means of accessing the innermost subconscious

Quiz 4 Answer Key

1. **(B)** Two office workers who eat in their own cubicles
2. **(D)** Scare the audience/reader
3. **(C)** Sublimination because of heavy censorship
4. **(A)** Intertextuality - Lewis Carrol's "Alice in Wonderland"
5. **(D)** Convey a sense of depth and resonance through references to earlier texts
6. **(C)** Dubious in its authenticity
7. **(A)** It is related to the oxygen - our source of breath
8. **(D)** Allegory denotes one specific meaning or message only whereas symbols can have a variety of interpretations
9. **(B)** Pattern recognition, symbolic reading, memory
10. **(B)** When a woman is offered the chance to relinquish her admission in a prestigious co-ed university in exchange for a full scholarship to another, all girls college
11. **(D)** A quest tale about a young girl who recognizes her own limitations and fears
12. **(D)** It describes two characters jointly sharing in an experience
13. **(B)** Capitalism
14. **(C)** He demonstrates selfish, exploitative tendencies
15. **(B)** Seasonal imagery in the poem that indicate the progression of human life
16. **(C)** Hansel & Gretel because of the trope of lost children
17. **(A)** Are accessible to a wider audience
18. **(A)** A character, Achilles' anger and response
19. **(D)** As a unifier, as a plot device, and as a means of conveying misery
20. **(D)** Rainbow appears after a refreshing rain
21. **(B)** A character's Lost Book is found in her dog's kennel, and reveals further lost household items
22. **(B)** Violence in literature is an act of aggression while not so in real life
23. **(A)** Macbeth,'s "Out out brief candle - " which points to the fragility of human existence
24. **(C)** It is conditioned by the historical state of affairs/events
25. **(B)** They symbolize the underworld and Greek mythology

How to Read Literature Like a Professor Bibliography

Sheza Alqera Atiq, author of ClassicNote. Completed on July 22, 2015, copyright held by GradeSaver.

Updated and revised by Aaron Suduiko October 7, 2015. Copyright held by GradeSaver.

Thomas C. Foster. How to Read Literature Like A Professor . New York: HarperCollins, 2003.

Armstrong, Nancy, and Leonard Tennenhouse. *The Violence of Representation (Routledge Revivals): Literature and the History of Violence*. Routledge, 2014.

Doob, Penelope Reed. *The idea of the labyrinth from classical antiquity through the Middle Ages*. Cornell Univ Pr, 1990.

Telotte, J. P. "A parasitic perspective: Romantic participation and Polidori's The Vampyre." *The blood is the life: Vampires in literature* (1999): 9-18.

Heldreth, Leonard G., and Mary Pharr, eds. *The blood is the life: vampires in literature*. Popular Press, 1999.

Ford, Boris, ed. *The age of Shakespeare*. Penguin books, 1982.

Jeffrey, David L. *A dictionary of biblical tradition in English literature*. Wm. B. Eerdmans Publishing, 1992.

Cirlot, J. C. *Dictionary of symbols*. Routledge, 2006.

Detweiler, Robert. "Christ and the Christ Figure in American Fiction." *The Christian Scholar* (1964): 111-124.

Woolf, Rosemary. "The Theme of Christ the Lover-Knight in Medieval English Literature." *The Review of English Studies* 13.49 (1962): 1-16.

Wilentz, Gay. "If You Surrender to the Air: Folk Legends of Flight and Resistance in African American Literature." *Melus* (1989): 21-32.

Blair, Kirstie. *Victorian Poetry and the Culture of the Heart*. Oxford University Press, 2006.

Linett, Maren. "Blindness and Intimacy in Early Twentieth-Century Literature."*Mosaic: a journal for the interdisciplinary study of literature* 46.3 (2013): 27-42.

McKee, John B. *Literary Irony and the Literary Audience, Studies in the Victimization of the Reader in Augustan Fiction.* Rodopi, 1974.

Victoria Best. "LitLove." 02/08/2010. <https://litlove.wordpress.com/2010/08/02/reading-at-table/>.

"NYTimes Bestseller." April 2015. <http://www.nytimes.com/best-sellers-books/>.

"ClassicLit." --. <http://classiclit.about.com/cs/productreviews/fr/aafpr_howtoread.htm>.

ClassicNotes

GrAdeSaver™

Getting you the grade since 1999™

Other ClassicNotes from GradeSaver™

Aristotle: Nicomachean Ethics
Aristotle's Poetics
Aristotle's Politics
Arms and the Man
A Room of One's Own
A Room With a View
A Rose For Emily and Other Short Stories
Around the World in 80 Days
A Sentimental Journey Through France and Italy
A Separate Peace
As I Lay Dying
A Streetcar Named Desire
Astrophil and Stella

A Study in Scarlet
As You Like It
A Tale of Two Cities
A Thousand Splendid Suns
Atlantia
Atlas Shrugged
Atonement
A Very Old Man With Enormous Wings
A Vindication of the Rights of Woman
A White Heron and Other Stories
A Wrinkle in Time
Babbitt
Balzac and the Little Chinese Seamstress
Bartleby the Scrivener

Bastard Out of Carolina
Beloved
Benito Cereno
Beowulf
Bhagavad-Gita
Billy Budd
Black Beauty
Black Boy
Blade Runner
Bleak House
Bless Me, Ultima
Blindness
Blood Meridian: Or the Evening Redness in the West
Blood Wedding
Bluest Eye
Brave New World
Breakfast at Tiffany's

For our full list of over 250 Study Guides, Quizzes,
Sample College Application Essays, Literature Essays and E-texts, visit:

www.gradesaver.com

ClassicNotes

Gr**A**deSaver™

Getting you the grade since 1999™

Other ClassicNotes from GradeSaver™

Breakfast of
   Champions
Burmese Days
By Night in Chile
Call of the Wild
Candide
Cannery Row
Casablanca
Catch-22
Catching Fire
Cathedral
Cat on a Hot Tin
   Roof
Cat's Cradle
Charlie and the
   Chocolate Factory
Charlotte's Web
Charlotte Temple
Childhood's End
Chinese Cinderella
Christina Rossetti:
   Poems

Christopher
   Marlowe's Poems
Chronicle of a Death
   Foretold
Citizen Kane
Civil Disobedience
Civilization and Its
   Discontents
Civil Peace
Cloud Atlas
Coleridge's Poems
Comedy of Errors
Communist
   Manifesto
Confessions
Confessions of an
   English Opium
   Eater
Connecticut Yankee
   in King Arthur's
   Court
Coriolanus
Crewel

Crime and
   Punishment
Cry, the Beloved
   Country
Cymbeline
Cyrano de Bergerac
Daisy Miller
David Copperfield
Death and the King's
   Horseman
Death and the
   Maiden
Death in Venice
Death of a Salesman
Democracy in
   America
Desire Under the
   Elms
Devil in a Blue
   Dress
Dharma Bums
Disgrace
Divergent

For our full list of over 250 Study Guides, Quizzes,
Sample College Application Essays, Literature Essays and E-texts, visit:

www.gradesaver.com

ClassicNotes

GradeSaver™

Getting you the grade since 1999™

Other ClassicNotes from GradeSaver™

Divine Comedy-I: Inferno
Do Androids Dream of Electric Sheep?
Doctor Faustus (Marlowe)
Don Quixote Book I
Don Quixote Book II
Dora: An Analysis of a Case of Hysteria
Dracula
Dr. Jekyll and Mr. Hyde
Dubliners
East of Eden
Edgar Huntly: Memoirs of a Sleep-Walker
Educating Rita
Electra by Sophocles

Emily Dickinson's Collected Poems
Emma
Ender's Game
Endgame
Enduring Love
Enrique's Journey
Equus
Esperanza Rising
Eternal Sunshine of the Spotless Mind
Ethan Frome
Eugene Onegin
Evelina
Everyday Use
Everyman: Morality Play
Everything is Illuminated
Exeter Book
Extremely Loud and Incredibly Close
Ezra Pound: Poems

Fahrenheit 451
Fallen Angels
Fear and Loathing in Las Vegas
Fences
Fifth Business
Fight Club
Fight Club (Film)
Flags of Our Fathers
Flannery O'Connor's Stories
Flight
Flowers for Algernon
For Colored Girls Who Have Considered Suicide When the Rainbow Is Enuf
For Whom the Bell Tolls
Founding Brothers
Frankenstein

For our full list of over 250 Study Guides, Quizzes,
Sample College Application Essays, Literature Essays and E-texts, visit:

www.gradesaver.com

ClassicNotes

GradeSaver™

Getting you the grade since 1999™

Other ClassicNotes from GradeSaver™

Franny and Zooey
Friday Night Lights
Fun Home
Gargantua and
  Pantagruel
Goethe's Faust
Gorilla, My Love
Go Tell it On the
  Mountain
Great Expectations
Grendel
Gulliver's Travels
Hamlet
Hard Times
Haroun and the Sea
  of Stories
Harry Potter and the
  Philosopher's
  Stone
Hatchet
Heart of Darkness
Hedda Gabler
Henry IV Part 1

Henry IV Part 2
Henry IV
  (Pirandello)
Henry V
Herzog
Hippolytus
Homo Faber
House of Mirth
House on Mango
  Street
Howards End
How the Garcia
  Girls Lost Their
  Accents
How to Read
  Literature Like a
  Professor
I, Claudius
I Know Why the
  Caged Bird Sings
Iliad
Incidents in the Life
  of a Slave Girl

In Cold Blood
Inherit the Wind
In Our Time
Insurgent
Interpreter of
  Maladies
In the Skin of a Lion
In the Time of the
  Butterflies
Into the Wild
Invisible Man
Ishmael
Island of the Blue
  Dolphins
I Will Marry When I
  Want
James and the Giant
  Peach
Jane Eyre
Jazz
John Donne: Poems
Johnny Tremain

For our full list of over 250 Study Guides, Quizzes,
Sample College Application Essays, Literature Essays and E-texts, visit:

www.gradesaver.com

ClassicNotes

GrΛdeSaver™

Getting you the grade since 1999™

Other ClassicNotes from GradeSaver™

Jorge Borges: Short
   Stories
Joseph Andrews
Jude the Obscure
Julius Caesar
Jungle of Cities
Juno and the
   Paycock
Kama Sutra
Kate Chopin's Short
   Stories
Keats' Poems and
   Letters
Kidnapped
King Lear
King Solomon's
   Mines
Kokoro
Kurt Vonnegut's
   Short Stories
Lady Chatterley's
   Lover

Lancelot: Or, the
   Knight of the Cart
Langston Hughes:
   Poems
Last of the
   Mohicans
Leaves of Grass
Left to Tell
Legend
Le Morte d'Arthur
Les Miserables
Letter From
   Birmingham Jail
Leviathan
Libation Bearers
Life is Beautiful
Life of Pi
Light In August
Like Water for
   Chocolate
Little Women
Lolita

Long Day's Journey
   Into Night
Look Back in Anger
Looking for Alaska
Lord Byron's Poems
Lord Jim
Lord of the Flies
Love in the Time of
   Cholera
Love Medicine
Lucy
Lying Awake
Macbeth
Madame Bovary
Maestro
Maggie: A Girl of
   the Streets and
   Other Stories
Manhattan Transfer
Mankind: Medieval
   Morality Plays
Mansfield Park
Mary Barton

For our full list of over 250 Study Guides, Quizzes,
Sample College Application Essays, Literature Essays and E-texts, visit:

www.gradesaver.com

ClassicNotes

GradeSaver™

Getting you the grade since 1999™

Other ClassicNotes from GradeSaver™

Master Harold...
   And the Boys
Matched
Matthew Arnold:
   Poems
MAUS
Measure for
   Measure
Medea
Merchant of Venice
Metamorphoses
Midaq Alley
Middlemarch
Middlesex
Midnight's Children
Moby Dick
Mockingjay
Moll Flanders
Monkey: A Folk
   Novel of China
Mother Courage and
   Her Children
Mrs. Dalloway

Mrs. Warren's
   Profession
Much Ado About
   Nothing
Murder in the
   Cathedral
My Antonia
Mythology
Narrative of the Life
   of Frederick
   Douglass
Native Son
Nervous Conditions
Never Let Me Go
New Introductory
   Lectures on
   Psychoanalysis
Nickel and Dimed:
   On (Not) Getting
   By in America
Night
Nine Stories
No Exit

No Longer at Ease
North and South
Northanger Abbey
Notes from
   Underground
Number the Stars
Oedipus Rex or
   Oedipus the King
Of Mice and Men
Oliver Twist
One Day in the Life
   of Ivan
   Denisovich
One Flew Over the
   Cuckoo's Nest
One Hundred Years
   of Solitude
On Liberty
On the Road
O Pioneers
Oroonoko
Oryx and Crake
Othello

For our full list of over 250 Study Guides, Quizzes,
Sample College Application Essays, Literature Essays and E-texts, visit:

www.gradesaver.com

ClassicNotes

GradeSaver™

Getting you the grade since 1999™

Other ClassicNotes from GradeSaver™

Our Town
Pale Fire
Pamela: Or Virtue
  Rewarded
Paper Towns
Paradise Lost
Peace Like a River
Pedro Paramo
Percy Shelley:
  Poems
Perfume: The Story
  of a Murderer
Persepolis: The
  Story of a
  Childhood
Persuasion
Phaedra
Phaedrus
Pilgrim's Progress
Poems of W.B.
  Yeats: The Rose
Poems of W.B.
  Yeats: The Tower

Poe's Poetry
Poe's Short Stories
Pope's Poems and
  Prose
Portrait of the Artist
  as a Young Man
Pride and Prejudice
Prometheus Bound
Pudd'nhead Wilson
Purple Hibiscus
Pygmalion
Rabbit, Run
Rashomon
Ray Bradbury: Short
  Stories
Rebecca
Regeneration
Return of the Native
Rhinoceros
Richard II
Richard III
Rip Van Winkle and
  Other Stories

Robert Browning:
  Poems
Robert Frost: Poems
Robinson Crusoe
Roll of Thunder,
  Hear My Cry
Roman Fever and
  Other Stories
Romeo and Juliet
Roots
Rosencrantz and
  Guildenstern Are
  Dead
Rudyard Kipling:
  Poems
Salome
Schindler's List
Season of Migration
  to the North
Second Treatise of
  Government
Secret Sharer

For our full list of over 250 Study Guides, Quizzes,
Sample College Application Essays, Literature Essays and E-texts, visit:

www.gradesaver.com

ClassicNotes

GradeSaver™

Getting you the grade since 1999™

Other ClassicNotes from GradeSaver™

Self Reliance and
  Other Essays
Sense and
  Sensibility
Shakespeare's
  Sonnets
Shantaram
She Stoops to
  Conquer
Short Stories of
  Ernest
  Hemingway
Short Stories of F.
  Scott Fitzgerald
Siddhartha
Silas Marner
Silence
Sir Gawain and the
  Green Knight
Sir Thomas Wyatt:
  Poems
Sister Carrie

Six Characters in
  Search of an
  Author
Slaughterhouse Five
Snow Country
Snow Falling on
  Cedars
Something Wicked
  This Way Comes
Song of Roland
Song of Solomon
Songs of Innocence
  and of Experience
Sonny's Blues
Sons and Lovers
Speak
Spenser's Amoretti
  and Epithalamion
Spring Awakening
Sula
Sundiata: An Epic of
  Old Mali
Sylvia Plath: Poems

Symposium by Plato
Tartuffe
Tell Me a Riddle
Tender is the Night
Tennyson's Poems
Tess of the
  D'Urbervilles
That Was Then, This
  is Now
The Absolutely True
  Diary of a Part-
  Time Indian
The Adventures of
  Augie March
The Adventures of
  Huckleberry Finn
The Adventures of
  Tom Sawyer
The Aeneid
The Age of
  Innocence
The Alchemist
  (Coelho)

For our full list of over 250 Study Guides, Quizzes,
Sample College Application Essays, Literature Essays and E-texts, visit:

www.gradesaver.com

ClassicNotes

GradeSaver™

Getting you the grade since 1999™

Other ClassicNotes from GradeSaver™

The Alchemist (Jonson)

The Ambassadors

The Analects of Confucius

The Arabian Nights: One Thousand and One Nights

The Autobiography of an Ex-Colored Man

The Awakening

The Bacchae

The Bean Trees

The Beggar's Opera

The Bell Jar

The Birthday Party

The Blithedale Romance

The Bloody Chamber

The Bonfire of the Vanities

The Book of Daniel

The Book of the Duchess and Other Poems

The Book Thief

The Boy in the Striped Pajamas

The Brief Wondrous Life of Oscar Wao

The Brothers Karamazov

The Burning Plain and Other Stories

The Canterbury Tales

The Caretaker

The Catcher in the Rye

The Caucasian Chalk Circle

The Cherry Orchard

The Chocolate War

The Chosen

The Chrysanthemums

The Circle

The Collector

The Color of Water

The Color Purple

The Consolation of Philosophy

The Coquette

The Count of Monte Cristo

The Country of the Pointed Firs and Other Stories

The Country Wife

The Cricket in Times Square

The Crucible

The Crying of Lot 49

The Curious Incident of the

For our full list of over 250 Study Guides, Quizzes,
Sample College Application Essays, Literature Essays and E-texts, visit:

www.gradesaver.com

ClassicNotes

GradeSaver™

Getting you the grade since 1999™

Other ClassicNotes from GradeSaver™

Dog in the Night-time

The Death of Ivan Ilych

The Devil and Tom Walker

The Devil's Arithmetic

The Diary of a Young Girl by Anne Frank

The Duchess of Malfi

The Electric Kool-Aid Acid Test

The English Patient

The Epic of Gilgamesh

The Eumenides

The Faerie Queene

The Fall of the House of Usher

The Fault in Our Stars

The Federalist Papers

The Five People You Meet in Heaven

The Fountainhead

The French Lieutenant's Woman

The Frogs

The Garden Party

The Giver

The Glass Castle

The Glass Menagerie

The Godfather

The God of Small Things

The Golden Ass

The Good Earth

The Good Woman of Setzuan

The Grapes of Wrath

The Great Gatsby

The Guest

The Handmaid's Tale

The Heart of the Matter

The Help

The Hiding Place

The History Boys

The History of Rasselas: Prince of Abissinia

The History of Tom Jones, a Foundling

The Hobbit

The Hot Zone

The Hound of the Baskervilles

The House of Bernarda Alba

For our full list of over 250 Study Guides, Quizzes, Sample College Application Essays, Literature Essays and E-texts, visit:

www.gradesaver.com

ClassicNotes

Getting you the grade since 1999™

ClassicNotes

GradeSaver™

Getting you the grade since 1999™

Other ClassicNotes from GradeSaver™

The Testing

The Theory of Moral Sentiments

The Things They Carried

The Threepenny Opera

The Time Machine

The Tortilla Curtain

The Trials of Brother Jero

The Truman Show

The Turn of the Screw

The Vicar of Wakefield

The Visit

The Wars

The Waste Land

The Watsons Go to Birmingham - 1963

The Wave

The Way of the World

The Wealth of Nations

The Whale Rider

The White Devil

The White Tiger

The Wind in the Willows

The Winter's Tale

The Woman Warrior

The Wonderful Wizard of Oz

The Yellow Wallpaper

The Young Elites

The Zoo Story

Things Fall Apart

Three Cups of Tea

Three Men in a Boat (To Say Nothing of the Dog)

Through the Looking Glass

Thus Spoke Zarathustra

Titus Andronicus

To Build a Fire

To Kill a Mockingbird

Top Girls

To the Lighthouse

Touching Spirit Bear

Treasure Island

Trifles

Troilus and Cressida

Tropic of Cancer

Tropic of Capricorn

Tuesdays With Morrie

Twelfth Night

Twilight

Ulysses

Uncle Tom's Cabin

For our full list of over 250 Study Guides, Quizzes, Sample College Application Essays, Literature Essays and E-texts, visit:

www.gradesaver.com

ClassicNotes

GrAdeSaver™

Getting you the grade since 1999™

Other ClassicNotes from GradeSaver™

Under the Feet of
  Jesus
Untouchable
Up From Slavery
Ursula Le Guin:
  Short Stories
Utilitarianism
Utopia
Vanity Fair
Villette
Volpone
Waiting for Godot
Waiting for Lefty
Walden
Walt Whitman:
  Poems
War and Peace
Washington Square

We
Weep Not, Child
What is the What
W. H. Auden:
  Poems
Where Are You
  Going, Where
  Have You Been?
Where the Red Fern
  Grows
White Fang
White Noise
White Teeth
Who's Afraid of
  Virginia Woolf
Wide Sargasso Sea
Wieland

Wilfred Owen:
  Poems
Winesburg, Ohio
Women in Love
Wonder
Wordsworth's
  Poetical Works
Woyzeck
Wuthering Heights
Year of Wonders
Yonnondio: From
  the Thirties
Young Goodman
  Brown and Other
  Hawthorne Short
  Stories
Zeitoun

For our full list of over 250 Study Guides, Quizzes,
Sample College Application Essays, Literature Essays and E-texts, visit:

www.gradesaver.com

Made in the USA
Columbia, SC
19 July 2019